Easy Enrichment IDEAS

Thinking Outside the Green Gelatin Box

EASY Enrichment IDEAS

Thinking Outside the Green Gelatin Box

By Trina Boice

Illustrated by Calvin Boice

spring creek
BOOK COMPANY
Provo, Utah

ISBN 13: 978-1-932898-28-6
ISBN 10: 1-932898-28-X
e. 1

Published by:
Spring Creek Book Company
P.O. Box 50355
Provo, Utah 84605-0355
www.springcreekbooks.com

Cover design © Spring Creek Book Company
Cover design by Nicole Cunningham
Inside illustrations © Calvin W. Boice III

Printed in the United States of America
10 9 8 7 6 5 4 3 2 1
Printed on acid-free paper

Library of Congress Cataloging-in-Publication Data
Boice, Trina, 1963-
  Easy enrichment ideas : thinking outside the green gelatin box / By Trina Boice.
     p. cm.
  ISBN-10: 1-932898-28-X (pbk. : alk. paper)
  ISBN-13: 978-1-932898-28-6 (pbk. : alk. paper)
  1. Family--Religious life. 2. Family--Religious aspects--Christianity. 3. Church of Jesus Christ
of Latter-day Saints--Doctrines. 4. Mormon Church--Doctrines. I. Title.

BX8643.F3B65 2005
249--dc22

                                    2004029293

Contents

CHAPTER ONE

Welcome to Enrichment Night!

No more wooden bunnies with fabric ears? Isn't that the first thought that flashed through your mind when you heard the announcement that the monthly Relief Society Homemaking Night was being replaced with Home, Family, and Personal Enrichment Meeting? Were you frightened or relieved? When I first heard the new—and long—name change, I wondered if the women on the General Relief Society Board in Salt Lake City had started drinking Coca-Cola with caffeine! Then as I pondered the new title I was pleased with the renewed focus and direction.

"The name 'Home, Family, and Personal Enrichment' is designed to communicate what this monthly Relief Society meeting can help us accomplish. The phrase 'personal enrichment' focuses our attention on the importance of first strengthening our sisters as individuals; then with that increased strength, they will be better able to build their family members, friends, neighbors, and community, with the ultimate goal of bringing each closer to our Heavenly Father and His Son, Jesus Christ." (Bonnie D. Parkin)

To enrich means to make rich or richer, especially by the addition or increase of some desirable quality, attribute, or ingredient. To enrich can also mean to improve the value of something by restoring what was once lost. Enriched bread is an example, and bread is exactly what we want to increase at our monthly meetings—the bread of life—Jesus Christ! While our attempts to create the most perfect wooden bunny were sometimes admirable, there is so much more that we can and should be doing. Don't get me wrong, I love a good craft class just as much as the next gal, but we live in perilous times when more demands are placed upon us and more is expected of us. We need a refuge from the storm and a place where we can gather renewed strength and direction. The changes for an "Enrichment Night" are to improve the value of how we sisters spend our time together each month. We should, quite literally, return to our homes enriched.

If you have been asked to plan and prepare this monthly event you have a sacred calling. The time spent at Enrichment Night is sacred. It is a time when a helpful wife and needed mother is called away from her home and family to spend an evening with you. That time, therefore, should be filled with meaningful activity and uplifting efforts that will enable her to return to her home an even better wife and mother. It is sacred time, because the women who will come to Enrichment Meeting often times will arrive with heavy hearts, burdened by the woes of the world, and it is your duty and privilege to lift their spirits and remind them the Lord is mindful of their needs, desires and responsibilities. It is sacred time because the Lord has much work for the sisters to do, and it is your privilege to give them tools and encouragement to do it. It is sacred time because the Lord has promised that wherever there are two or more gathered in His name there He will be also. (Matthew 18:20)

The goal for every program and auxiliary in the Church is to "Come unto Christ." Home, Family, and Personal Enrichment Meetings can help sisters find something each month in which they might improve and come closer to Christ. The meeting is designed to help sisters build spiritual strength, develop personal skills, strengthen the home and family, and provide gospel service (see *Church Handbook of Instructions, Book 2: Priesthood and Auxiliary Leaders* [1998], 202).

As you and the other leaders in your Relief Society plan these meetings pray about the sisters in your ward and thoughtfully consider their needs. You have a stewardship over them now and have the right to receive revelation about how you can best serve them and help them become the women the Lord knows they can become. Talk with your Relief Society presidency and Bishopric to see if they have specific topics they know need to be covered in an Enrichment lesson or class.

When planning your classes and activities, be mindful of the single sisters, widows, single mothers and those who have been unable to bear children. Their hearts are especially heavy and they need the great sisterhood that can be found in the Relief Society. Be sensitive to their special needs and try to always offer classes they can participate in that don't make them feel singled out.

It's helpful to have all of the sisters in your ward fill out some kind of interest and talent survey to direct your energies towards classes that will be useful and immediately applicable to your specific Relief Society. Find out what talents your sisters have and which women would feel comfortable sharing their skills with a group as a teacher. Every sister has a talent to share! Inviting sisters to teach a class or make a special presentation at Enrichment Night is a terrific way to help each sister shine in front of the others. Esteem will improve both for self and others.

This book is meant to be a big brainstorm of ideas. Hopefully the suggestions will trigger your own creative brainstorm. Adjust the ideas on these pages to suit the needs and interests of your Relief Society sisters. Mix and match. The activities in this book include a catchy (and hopefully clever) name for a class that could be offered or to use as a theme for the entire evening during Enrichment Night. Feel free to get your own creative juices flowing and think up your own. The trick is to design an evening that is intriguing and creative so that sisters will want to find out more by attending. Your flyers and posters should advertise just enough information to whet the sisters' appetite and to convince them that through their attendance at Enrichment Night they will be filled.

This book is to get you to think outside the box...that green gelatin box we Mormon gals tend to stay in due to habit and tradition. (They say that Utah is the Jell-O capital of the United States.) There's a whole world of exciting classes and activities out there! There's so much to learn and do and be! If you don't have someone in your ward who could teach your sisters a certain skill consider inviting an expert in your community to attend your Enrichment Night and share his or her talents with the sisters. Invite someone famous or your neighbor down the street. Invite a movie star or a Congressman or anyone you want. Shoot for the stars! Your sisters deserve the best. Raise the bar. Expect more. Magnify your calling. Enrich your sisters.

Let me say one more thing about those wooden bunnies with fabric ears. A lot of bonding can occur during craft classes, and I'm not just talking about glue. There can be a fun camaraderie while working on crafts together. While your efforts should be to offer classes with great substance and helpful information to meet the needs of the sisters, there is still a place for creative arts in Enrichment Night, especially when accompanied by an inspiring mini-lesson that teaches meaningful application of that new skill.

I remember when I was a little girl and would accompany my mother to her mid-week Relief Society meetings. (Am I dating myself?) One day she came home with three beautiful wise men she had made, using rich fabrics and interesting accessories. I remember being so impressed with her talents and was proud that she had made them all by herself for us to use as a Christmas decoration in our home. They helped me focus on the story of the Savior's birth when I looked at them and there was something magical about their faces that said to me "Wise men still seek Him."

Every year my mother still sets out those wise men on her table at Christmas time and that same flood of awe and admiration come over me. There can be great testimony in glue guns! Heavenly Father spent six days creating lovely things. Like His works, be sure they have important value! Our homes should be filled, not with meaningless trinkets, but with things that cause us to reflect on the Savior. May you be blessed in your good efforts to enrich the lives of your Relief Society sisters!

CHAPTER TWO
"The Errand of Angels"

Relief Society sisters are known for the many casseroles and quilts that we produce. Women in the Relief Society have always gathered to lift one another and reach out to those in need ever since its conception. On March 17, 1842 the prophet, Joseph Smith, first organized the "Female Relief Society of Nauvoo."

There were twenty women who gathered in the upper room of the Red Brick Store in Nauvoo, Illinois to learn how they could serve more effectively. They had organized themselves to make shirts for the men who were building the temple and they wanted to do more to help. They presented Joseph with a Constitution they had written so they could form a "Ladies' Society."

Joseph praised their good desires but told him he had something greater planned for them. He told them he would organize the sisters "under the priesthood after a pattern of the priesthood."

Later he said, "The Church was never perfectly organized until the women were thus organized." (*History of Relief Society*, p. 18) Emma Hale Smith was elected to be president. She chose Elizabeth Ann Whitney and Sarah M. Cleveland to be her counselors. Eliza R. Snow was appointed to be secretary. That small gathering was the beginning of what is now the largest women's organization in the world, the Relief Society of the Church of Jesus Christ of Latter-day Saints.

The prophet stated that the purposes of the Society were as follows: "that the Society of sisters might provoke the brethren to good works in looking to the wants of the poor—searching after objects of charity, and in administering to their wants—to assist by correcting the morals and strengthening the virtues of the community." (*Minutes of the Female Relief Society of Nauvoo*, March 17, 1842, p.13.) Home, Family and Personal Enrichment Meeting should be an extension of those efforts.

The Church grew quickly and the Relief Society presidency had a stewardship to care for all of the members. One year later, in July 1843, a committee consisting of four women was appointed in each ward to visit and assess the needs of the members, solicit contributions from Church members, and to assist those who were in need of help. This was the start of the visiting teaching program, which is still in place today.

At the ninth meeting of the Relief Society in Nauvoo, Illinois, the Prophet Joseph Smith quoted the Savior: "Said Jesus, 'Ye shall do the work, which ye see me do.' These are the grand keywords for the society to act upon." (*History of the Church*, 5:20.) An official monthly "homemaking" meeting wasn't established in the Relief Society for many years, but sisters gathered together to teach one another and serve where they could.

After settling in the Salt Lake Valley sixteen women met together weekly as members of the "Indian Relief Society" to befriend and make clothes for the Indians. In 1854 Brigham Young encouraged each ward to form its own "Indian Relief Society." The sisters then extended their efforts to include caring for the poor in their wards and providing meetinghouse carpets and supplies for handcart companies. I love the story that tells when sisters heard an announcement in General Conference about some of the Saints who were caught by early snows in the mountains they stripped off their petticoat stockings right there in the Tabernacle and piled them into the wagons to send to their freezing brothers and sisters. Now that's enthusiastic service!

In 1866 Eliza R. Snow became President of the Relief Society and was asked to provide a "Constitution" for all local units, uniting them in name, purpose, and organization. She later helped create a magazine for the sisters and called it the "Women's Exponent." Under the direction of Brigham Young, the Deseret Silk Association was organized and he encouraged the growing, harvesting, and spinning of silk as a homemaking skill that Relief Society sisters were called upon to learn and assist in its efforts. Later he appointed Emmeline B. Wells to head up a grain storage program and Relief Society sisters were enlisted to help with this project as well.

The women of the Church also kept busy caring for the health and wellness of each other and their non-member neighbors. The Relief Society opened the Deseret Hospital and sisters were taught skills to help with medical needs.

In 1902 the first Relief Society handbook was published with Mother Education lessons, focusing on child child-rearing ideas. In 1914 the "Relief Society Magazine" was created with standardized lesson plans on theological, cultural and homemaking topics were introduced by the general Relief Society board members. The lessons were to be taught on a rotating monthly schedule with each topic being assigned to a particular week in the month. Nursing classes were also offered under the title "The Relief Society School of Obstetrics and Nursing" until 1920 when arrangements were made with LDS Hospital for those who wished to continue their training. General Relief Society President Emmeline B. Wells felt passionately that Latter-day Saint women should be "the best informed of any women on the face of the earth." Bushels of wheat were sent to survivors of the 1906 San Francisco earthquake and after World War 1 the Relief Society sold 200,000 bushels of wheat to the U.S. government. A "Wheat Trust Fund" was established for the purpose of purchasing more wheat in the future and interest from that Fund was used to sponsor hundreds of health clinics for expectant mothers, babies, and preschool children. Much later, thousands of bushels of wheat and nearly two million dollars in assets were transferred to the First Presidency for use in the Welfare program.

It was during this time that the Relief Society created the motto that still represents the Relief Society today: "Charity Never Faileth." A Relief Society Guide was created which outlined four meetings per month.

When the Church Welfare Plan was established the Relief Society was given the main responsibility for preserving food, providing clothing and bedding, and teaching welfare principles to the sisters. The Relief Society served wherever it could to help humanity recover from two world wars and a national economic depression. Relief Society sisters struggled to make ends meet during those difficult times and so the "Women's Commission House" (today called "Mormon Handicraft") was created in Salt Lake City to help women at home earn money by selling their home-made goods on consignment.

During World War II sisters were encouraged to donate their time to the Red Cross as well as local welfare assignments. They sent clothing, food and thousands of quilts to help the Saints in Europe and Japan. By the 1960s Relief Society materials were being sent into many other countries and printed in foreign languages.

Relief Society meetings were held during the daytime in the middle of the week In 1971 all LDS sisters over the age of 18 were included in the Relief Society membership, which exceeded one million. The first general women's fireside was held in 1978 and is still an annual tradition enjoyed worldwide. At that meeting President Kimball implored Relief Society sisters to become scholars of the scriptures.

In the 1980s the focus of Relief Society action was aimed at the local ward levels and Stake Relief Society boards were eliminated. Flexibility and simplicity were guidelines. All sisters were encouraged to find opportunities for service, learning, sisterhood and spirituality.

President Gordon B. Hinckley instructed Barbara W. Winder, when he issued her call as Relief Society General President, that her presidency would be for "a different time."

For the first time, General Presidents of the Relief Society, Young

Women, and Primary traveled together internationally to make the auxiliaries more effective in bringing women and their children to Christ. The consolidated church schedule was also introduced which created a three hour block of Church meetings on Sundays with one hour reserved for Relief Society lessons. A Homemaking evening once a month was created for sisters to attend other classes and activities.

In the 1990s the family began to be under attack more than ever. A Relief Society Declaration was created, affirming the divine role of women. It states:

We are beloved spirit daughters of God,
and our lives have meaning, purpose, and direction.
As a worldwide sisterhood, we are united in our devotion
to Jesus Christ, our Savior and Exemplar.
We are women of faith, virtue, vision, and charity who:

Increase our testimonies of Jesus Christ
through prayer and scripture study.

Seek spiritual strength by following the
promptings of the Holy Ghost.

Dedicate ourselves to strengthening
marriages, families, and homes.

Find nobility in motherhood and joy in womanhood.

Delight in service and good works.

Love life and learning.

Stand for truth and righteousness.

Sustain the priesthood as the authority of God on earth.

Rejoice in the blessings of the temple,
understand our divine destiny,
and strive for exaltation.

To celebrate the end of the twentieth century, hundreds of Relief Society sisters contributed more than 1,999 hours of service to humanitarian projects in one evening! What a fitting event for an organization that was born out of the desire to serve others by a few dear sisters.

Effective on the first day of January 2000, the monthly "Homemaking Night" was changed to "Home, Family and Personal Enrichment" in order to better instruct and edify the vast needs of the nearly four million members of the Relief Society in over 160 countries worldwide. Sherri L. Dew's statement crystallized the importance of the changes when she said "We no longer have the luxury of spending our energy on anything that does not lead us and our families to Christ."

In the guidelines we read that its purpose is to build spiritual strength, develop personal skills, strengthen home and family, and provide gospel service. Enrichment Evening should be a sanctuary where friends come together to both give and receive. Our sisterhood is a great blessing and makes our lives richer, indeed.

CHAPTER THREE

Enrichment Night Guidelines

The Relief Society presidency and the Home, Family, and Personal Enrichment Leader should prayerfully plan the monthly meetings while considering the specific needs of the women in their ward or branch.

Virginia U. Jensen explains, "Home, Family and Personal Enrichment is a place for us to share sisterhood, to gain knowledge, to learn skills, and to increase testimony. This meeting is also the place to rededicate ourselves to our homes and families and to the giving of service wherever it is needed."

Enrichment Meeting should include the following format:

- **Relief Society President's report**. The president or one of her counselors could share information about service opportunities, discuss ward business or talk about any other non-confidential concerns from the most recent ward council meeting that your bishop would like all sisters to be aware of that month. Relief Society sisters will rise to the occasion when called upon to offer help and ideas. They are a tremendous resource for your ward.

- **Topic presentation.** This segment should be a 15-minute presentation on a designated spiritual topic. The Church suggests the following ten topics:
    —Spiritual Development
    —Homemaking Skills
    —Marriage and Family Relations
    —Strengthening Relationships
    —Self-Reliance
    —Service
    —Physical and Emotional Health
    —Personal Development and Education
    —Literacy
    —Cultural Arts

    Because there are twelve months in the year and only ten designated topics, you and your leaders should choose two other topics based on the specific needs of your Relief Society sisters. You may want to plan a different kind of Enrichment Meeting to commemorate the birthday of the Relief Society in March or a special evening during December to celebrate Christmas or anything else you think your sisters would be benefited by.

- **Activity Segment.** This is a 60- to 90-minute segment of the evening, during which practical skills that apply to the spiritual topic are taught or service activities are held. You could offer several mini-classes for the sisters to choose from or set up stations that everyone could rotate through so they can enjoy them all! Use lots of variety to keep the sisters coming back for more each month, such as workshops, discussions, role-play, media presentations, hands-on experiences, guest speakers, etc. There are so many great things to learn and do!

- Refreshments or light meal. Treat the sisters to something yummy, share recipes, offer healthy alternatives to decadent desserts, teach the women how to present a lovely table and enjoy the taste of good company!

May the Lord bless you in your efforts to create a lovely evening for your sisters where testimonies will be strengthened, friendships renewed, skills enhanced, service rendered, hearts warmed, and where the Spirit of Christ will fill their souls. I hope you find the ideas in this book to be easy and enriching!

CHAPTER FOUR

Spiritual Development

D&C 88:63 "Draw near unto me and I will draw near unto you; seek me diligently and ye shall find me; ask, and ye shall receive; knock, and it shall be opened unto you."

TEMPLE WORSHIP

"HEAVENLY KNOT TYING"

Moderate a group discussion about the blessings of the temple. Make a Family Home Evening packet with pictures children can color for visual aids that show blessings we receive when we are worthy to go to the temple. Have sisters share experiences of how temple attendance has blessed their families. Create a wall hanging that says something like "Families Can Be Together Forever."

"CELESTIAL RSVP"

Discuss how to prepare spiritually for temple participation. If your ward has a Temple Preparation class you could invite that teacher to share some of his/her experiences while teaching the course and what it is he/she does to help prepare members of the church to enter the temple. The teacher could share highlights of the course, sign sisters up to attend lessons on Sunday and answer questions about who to talk to about starting the recommend process. By the end of the lesson, sisters will be able to understand the Lord's invitation to go to His holy house and be able to RSVP and say, "Yeah, I'm going to the temple!"

"SEW BEAUTIFUL"

Sew temple dresses. Teach how wedding dresses could be altered tastefully to wear inside the temple. You could even have a temple dress fashion show. Be mindful of sisters who haven't yet gone to the temple. You could even sew baptism clothing to donate to your ward's missionary efforts.

"E-TERNAL"

Get it? Share computer links that can help you link your family for eternity! Teach the sisters how to submit names for the Temple Ready program. Take a tour of the Family History Center and learn how to use PAF, Gedcom, and other computer resources. Encourage each sister to bring a name to prepare for temple work. Your Relief Society could set a goal to create a "Relief Society in heaven" by preparing names and doing temple work for enough women to form a "heavenly" group of Relief Society sisters!

"WITHIN THE FRAMEWORK OF THE GOSPEL"

Frame pictures of temples, prophets, Church sites, or Christ for each child's bedroom, a husband's office, over a fireplace or other places of honor in your home or as gifts. Learn how to build frames out of beautiful wood or other interesting crafting material. You could also buy inexpensive frames and learn a fun faux painting technique to dress up the frame. This class could also teach sisters creative matting designs for frames of all sizes.

"GETTING THE HANG OF IT" OR "HANG ON"

Make white coat hangers with crochet or satin fabric where sisters could hang their temple dresses to remind them to "HANG on to their Standards and Covenants."

Make wall hangings with images of temples or other gospel designs.

"CELESTIAL SISTERS"

Plan a special day or night when sisters can perform temple work together in the temple. This could take the place of Enrichment Night one month or could be offered as an additional activity for sisters during a month when your Relief Society wants to emphasize increased temple attendance. Arrange a special chapel session or to have someone in the temple presidency speak to the sisters.

"I'VE GOT YOU COVERED"

Make temple shawls to donate to the temple or for your sisters to use while inside the temple when they get a little chilled. This would be a great project if your sisters want to learn how to knit or crochet. You may want to check with the temple first to see if they have patterns or size restrictions.

"A NOSE FOR NEEDLEWORK" OR
"A HANKERING FOR A HANKY"

Embroider handkerchiefs that could be used at temple dedications, baptisms, as wedding gifts or for any other special occasion. Offer to make handkerchiefs for the Young Women to take to the temple when they are old enough. This is a great project to work on to teach women how to do tatting. You could also talk about vintage fabrics and how to make lace. A prayer handkerchief is a tradition brought to this country prior to the Revolution and is supposed to be a message of love and comfort when given to another person.

"TEMPLE TAPESTRY"

Sew or embroider a packet for temple clothing. There are some beautiful embroidery designs you can buy on software for special sewing machines that stitch the temple of your choosing onto fabric. You could also stitch the temple designs on other fabric for pillow cases at home, wall hangings or clothing. Sisters could also learn how to do lacework.

"COUNTED CROSS STITCH CRAFTS"

Show sisters how to make different kinds of items using cross-stitch techniques. Make a temple recommend holder or offer to make special forms to cover tissue boxes for the temple. Recommends can be simply kept in your wallet or in a special place like a cross stitch holder for your temple clothing bag. You could also make a holder to keep the temple schedule in or a refrigerator magnet with the phone number for the nearest temple and its operating hours. Design a picture for your wall that says your family motto or something like "Families Can Be Together Forever."

"FAMILY FRAMEWORK"

Make a frame to go around a special picture of you or your family at the temple. It could be a picture of your closest temple, the one you were married in, your favorite temple in the world, or a picture of you standing outside the temple where your family was sealed together! There are many crafting techniques you could use to build your own frame, using special wood cutouts. You could decoupage temple pictures onto a frame, use different faux painting techniques, make a fabric-padded frame or incorporate any style your sisters are interested in learning how to make.

"SPIRITUAL MOUNTAINTOPS" OR
"DOTTING THE EARTH"

Learn about the temples all over the world. As you display pictures of all of the temples you could design a quiz to see how many of the temples class participants recognize and then share some facts about each one. Create a "Temple Trivia" game that sisters could play and then take home to share with their families for Family Home Evening. Invite sisters to talk about different temples they have visited. Learn about the different kinds of architecture and exterior symbolism that are used in temples today. You could also have the ladies put red dots on a map of the world to show how temples are beginning to dot the earth, as was prophesied.

"HIGH ON A MOUNTAIN TOP" OR
"PATRONS AND MATRONS"

Invite the temple president and his wife who preside over the nearest temple to speak to the sisters about the history of that temple. Have them share what their typical day is like working inside the temple and serving in this area. Have someone perform the song "High On A Mountain Top."

"TEMPLE MOUNT" OR "WESTERN WALL"

Study the Temples of Solomon and Herod. Read Old Testament accounts of how they were built, the dimensions and contents as well as the symbolism associated with them. Discuss how our temples are similar and different today. Talk about what lessons the Lord wanted to teach the children of Israel and how we can apply those lessons today. Show pictures and video footage of what the area looks like today. Invite someone who has traveled to Jerusalem to share his/her experiences.

"TEMPLES AND TABERNACLES"

Learn about the Tabernacle in the Wilderness that was used by the children of Israel. Read Old Testament accounts of how it was built, the importance of the Ark of the Covenant, the staff of Aaron, manna, shewbread, the tablets, and other items that were contained within. Talk about how the children of Israel used it and what lessons we can learn from it. Create visual aids or a Family Home Evening packet that the sisters could take home to teach their families about the Tabernacle and the Lord's temples.

"WHERE JESUS WALKED"

Invite someone who has traveled to the Holy Land to share photos, slides, and souvenirs from the trip and talk about places where Jesus would have walked. There are some great videos that show the sacred city and explain how the sites and remains have important significance to several religions. Discuss prophecies that have and will be fulfilled in that land, current international events, and scriptures that talk about specific locations.

"THE TRIUMPHANT SHOUT" OR "GREAT REJOICING"

Tell several faith-promoting stories about temple dedications throughout the world. The dedication of the Kirtland temple in particular had some wondrous events that are inspiring and build testimony. Share feelings about when the Nauvoo or Palmyra temples were built. Learn about the dedicatory prayer that was offered for the temple closest to your church building. If you're really lucky and have one in your area, you could attend a temple Open House together for Enrichment Night.

"CALENDAR CREATOR"

Create special calendars for the upcoming year that have pictures of different temples for each month and include a written reminder of the operating hours for your closest temple. Organize car pools for ward temple day or create a babysitting club that sisters could use to help each other out. You could present a calendar that the sisters could use to coordinate caring for each other's children or driving to the temple together. Organize a dessert social after ward temple night.

"THE SONGS OF THE RIGHTEOUS"

Learn songs about the temple. There are some great ones in the hymnal with accompanying scriptures and there is also a good book that explains the history of each of the hymns that could add further insight. It would be sweet to invite a few children to sing some of the Primary songs about temples. Have sisters learn the Primary song "I love to see the temple." Talk about why and how music helps us feel the Spirit.

"PRECIOUS PLASTER"

Create a replica of a temple in clay, plaster, cross-stitch, sugar cubes, cross stitch, Legos, bread dough, or through some other interesting medium. (I know, you're having visions of that scene in the movie "The RM" where one sister carves an ice sculpture of the SLC temple with a chain saw!) The Relief Society could even sponsor an art contest for the Primary, Young Men and Young Women with all entries based on a temple theme. Prizes could be awarded and artwork showcased at Enrichment Night and later hung somewhere in your church building for all to enjoy. Encourage sisters to display pictures of the temple in their homes. The Relief Society could present a special picture of the temple to each sister as a gift around Christmas time or during the Relief Society birthday celebration.

"SQUEAKY CLEAN"

Go to the temple and wash the windows of all the cars in the parking lot and leave a loving note on the windshield, thanking the patrons for their service in the temple that day. Sit on the lawn near the temple and talk about the importance of being spiritually clean.

"PARADE OF PAPER" OR "GOSPEL GRATITUDE"

Write thank you letters to the temple presidency for their service. You could use this time to also teach sisters how to make different kinds of paper for note cards or stationery. Write "thank you" letters to the young men and young women for their temple service when they go to the temple to perform proxy ordinance work.

"THE FEATHER OF PEACE"

Have someone teach a class about how we can make our homes feel the peace that is felt inside the temple. Relate the Quaker story about the feather of peace and how the spirit can bless our home. Talk about all of the traditions families can have to create a loving atmosphere. Share ideas of how sisters can create feelings of peace in their neighborhoods and communities.

"SACRED SEALS"

Invite a young couple who has recently been married in the temple to share some of their experiences about temple marriage. This would be a great class to invite the young women in the ward to attend with their mothers. Display pictures of other ward members who were married in temples. Sisters could decorate the room by displaying their wedding dresses and temple photos. Invite a family who has recently been sealed in the temple to talk about that special day.

"SHOWER HER WITH LOVE"

Throw a bridal shower for sisters who will be getting married in the temple soon. You could also offer classes on other aspects of how to throw a shower such as invitations, party games, themes, favors, gift ideas, photography, and thank you cards. Focus on the importance of getting married in the temple to the right person at the right time.

"TEMPLE PAGEANT"

If one is available in your area, attend a Temple Pageant together as a Relief Society. Most are held during summer months, but a few are offered during other seasons such as Easter and Christmas. Get directions and scheduled times on-line. Some shows include the Mesa Easter Pageant, "And It Came To Pass" Oakland temple pageant, Hill Cumorah Pageant in Palmyra, New York, "The Mormon Miracle" in Manti, Utah, "City of Gathering" in Kirtland, Ohio. If you don't live close to any pageants you could show a video of the performance.

PERSONAL PRAYER

"SACRED SPACE"

Discuss different ways to pray: in public, through meditation, through song, aloud, on knees, in the shower, while driving a car, in our "closets," as mouthpiece for a group, etc. Talk about how to make our conversations with Heavenly Father more meaningful and how we can create "sacred spaces" in our homes and lives.

"PRAYER POWER"

Create a prayer journal and talk about how to use one to help recognize how the Lord is blessing you in your life. Special petitions to the Lord could be recorded in a journal and then when you see those prayers being answered you write down how He blessed you or unfolded His will to you. You can also write about specific promptings you felt during prayer, as well as feelings you experienced while talking with Heavenly Father.

Oftentimes a prayer journal will help you discern how the spirit works in your life and just how often the Lord answers even the smallest prayer. Discuss how to be more specific in our prayers so that it's easier to see and recognize the answers to our prayers. Did you know George Washington kept a prayer journal!

"PRAYERS AND PETITIONS"

Study different prayers that were used in the scriptures such as David's Psalms, when Enos prayed, Christ's prayer in Gethsemane, when Moses prayed for God's presence, when Alma prayed for his son, etc. Learn about the Presidential Prayer Team, National Day of Prayer, famous prayers such as the "Lord's Prayer" by St. Francis of Assisi, and local and national events your sisters could get involved with to pray for others.

Help new sisters know how to submit names to the temple prayer roll and talk about the roles that faith, authority, and inspiration play in special prayers such as a Father's blessing or blessing upon the sick.

"PRAYER ROCKS!" OR "SPIRITUAL STONES"

Have sisters decorate prayer rocks for themselves, for the family, or to give as gifts with the attached poem:

I'm your little Prayer Rock
And this is what I'll do,
Just put me on your pillow
'Til the day is through.
Then turn back the covers
And climb into your bed
And whack! Your little Prayer Rock
Will hit you on the head
Then you will remember
To get up, say your prayers.
This is how you'll find the truth
Of what I have to say.

Then when you are finished
Just dump me on the floor.
I'll stay there through the night-time
To give you help once more.
When your sleep is over
Clunk! I'll stub your toe,
So you will remember
Your prayers before you go.

Return me to your pillow
When your bed is made
And your little Prayer Rock
Will continue in your aid.
Because your Heavenly Father
Desires for you to know
The answer to your questions
And the way for you to go.

"SACRED SACRAMENTS"

Study the Sacrament prayers. Discuss ways sisters can partake of the Sacrament in more meaningful ways. Share ideas on how to help younger children be reverent during the Sacrament. You could even show sisters how to make "Quiet Books" for their children to use during Sacrament meetings.

"PRAYER PRETZELS"

Learn how to make pretzels to eat and share the story about pretzels and prayer: In about 610 A.D. a creative Alpine Monk decided to make use of pieces of dough left over from baking bread. The monk formed them into thin strips folded into a looped twist to represent the folded arms of children in prayer.

This yummy treat was given to the children as they learned their prayers. They began calling the treat "Pretiola," which is Latin for "little reward." Soon it was known all over the world as a pretzel.

"BROTHER JOSEPH"

This would be a great class to have when the course of study for Sunday School is the Doctrine & Covenants and members are studying church history. Read Joseph Smith 2:8-15 and discuss the preparation that took place before that great prayer which began the restoration of the gospel. Talk about how we can better prepare ourselves to commune with the Lord. Discuss other moments of prayer and petition that opened the heavens and resulted in other revelations in the Doctrine and Covenants.

"DOXOLOGY 101"

(The sisters will go to this class just to find out what that word means!) Study the Lord's prayer. Read and discuss Matthew 6:9-13. Talk about the Lord's formula for prayer. Learn about different kinds of prayers and blessings such as how and when to dedicate a home, temple dedications, Father's blessings, at the opening session of Congress, graduation Baccalaureate, baby blessings, etc. Talk about how such prayers could be recorded in journals and when it is appropriate to tape record special prayers or blessings.

"DIVINE COMMUNICATION"

Learn about the language of prayer and how to use such words as thee, thy, thine, thou, etc. Discuss how people pray in other languages, using formal and familiar verbage. Talk about how to show more reverence and respect in our prayers. Talk about the different forms of conjugation that are used to pray in other languages. Discuss proper religious behavior when sisters are around people of other faiths and cultures.

PERSONAL SCRIPTURE STUDY

"SMART CHARTS"

Design creative charts to help sisters record their daily scripture study. You could even print out special coupons or certificates with awards for reading a certain number of days in a row. Your Relief Society might even choose to reward little pieces of candy, stickers, or other things to sisters who reach their reading goals each month. Let your sisters know you support their efforts to study the scriptures more! You could also design scripture timeline charts by rolling out large butcher paper and recording important events in church history or the life of a prophet or a period of time that is being studied in Sunday School.

"FEAST ON THE WORD"

Have a lesson and "Taster's Table" of foods from the Bible. Create special dishes using dates, figs, olives, etc. You could also have a "Smell Session" where sisters could smell common Bible fragrances such as frankincense, myrrh, cardamom, etc. Share recipes so the sisters can make scripture meals at home for their families. Have sisters bake this "Scripture Cake":

Ingredients:

3/4 cup Genesis 18:8

1 1/2 cup Jeremiah 6:20

5 Isaiah 10:14 (separated)

3 cups sifted Leviticus 24:5

3 teaspoons 2 Kings 2:20
3 teaspoons Amos 4:5
1 teaspoon Exodus 3:23
1/4 teaspoon each 2 Chronicles 9:9
1/2 cup Judges 4:19
3/4 cup chopped Genesis 43:11
3/4 cup finely cut Jeremiah 24:5
3/4 cup 2 Samuel 16:1
Whole Genesis 43:11

Cream Genesis 18 with Jeremiah 6. Beat in yolks of Isaiah 10, one at a time. Sift together Leviticus 24; 2 Kings 2; Amos 4; Exodus 30; and 2 Chronicles 9. Blend into creamed mixture alternately with Judges 4. Beat whites of Isaiah 10 till stiff; fold in. Fold in chopped Genesis 43; Jeremiah 24; and 2 Samuel 16. Turn into 10 inch tube pan that has been greased and dusted with Leviticus 24. Bake at 325 degrees F until it is golden brown or Gabriel blows his trumpet, whichever happens first. Bake for an hour and ten minutes. Remove from oven. Cool, serve and enjoy!

"WHO'S WHO"

Learn about Who's Who in the scriptures so sisters become more familiar with names. There are some great books that list all of the names and where they are found in the standard works, their contributions and what we can learn from them.

"SISTER SCRIPTORIANS"

Have someone show the sisters all of the resources that are available to improve their personal scripture study such as Institute and Seminary manuals, reference books, Scripture commentary books, maps, Topical Guide & Index, scripture study shows on BYUTV, Church videos, Internet resources, etc.

Play "Scripture Charades." Teach them rhyming tricks to remember the names of the book in the Bible or how to memorize certain passages.

"SCRIPTURE STUDIES" OR "INSPIRATIONAL INK"

Create a scripture journal and talk about how to use one. You could decorate special books or binders where feelings can be recorded during scripture study. Encourage sisters to write their testimonies and favorite scripture verses in their journals. This could be a beautiful gift for others as well as become a cherished family heirloom.

"BIBLE BOOKMARKS"

Make pretty bookmarks the sisters could use in their scriptures or give as gifts. Teach the sisters some new technique such as using dried flowers, rubber stamping, gold embossing, or some other crafting technique that they are interested in learning how to do. Bookmarks make great gifts for Visiting Teachers, children's Sunday School teachers, Home Teachers, and baptism gifts.

"ON THE MARK"

Invite a Seminary or Institute teacher to show different ways sisters could mark their scriptures such as color coding, using the missionary discussion marking system, stick-on scripture pictures, Seminary Scripture Mastery style or design your own system such as marking all scriptures that talk about charity or missionary work or the importance of families. Have sisters bring their scriptures to mark while listening to nice music or while watching a Conference Talk about the importance of scriptures.

Prepare copies of the Book of Mormon by highlighting certain key scriptures and then give them to your ward missionaries to share with their investigators.

"QUEST FOR QUIET TIME"

Have someone suggest creative ways to find more time during our busy days to read and study the scriptures, such as in the car while waiting to pick up your children from their activities, in the doctor's office, listening to scriptures on tape while cooking, etc. Give a prize to the sister who can think of the most creative way to incorporate scripture study into her life!

"LDS PDA ASAP" OR "CYBER SCRIPTURES"

Have someone teach the sisters how to download the scriptures onto their PDA's and home computers and beam helpful scriptures to one another. Learn about study guides and resources on the Internet.

"DISCOVERING GOD'S WORD" OR "MY WALK WITH THE LORD"

Invite a local Institute or Seminary teacher to speak about the importance of daily scripture study. The teacher could share some insights into the scriptures that are being studied this year. Discuss the importance of applying the scriptures to our lives.

"MESMERIZING, MEMORIZING MOMS"

Have Seminary parents set a goal to memorize all of the same Scripture Mastery verses that their children are learning in Seminary this year. Make creative posters and charts to help them memorize. Offer prizes to sisters who achieve their goals! Invite a Seminary teacher to show you memorizing tricks. Hold a Scripture Chase event with the sisters.

"ENSIGN TO THE NATIONS"

Offer a class where articles from the Ensign are discussed and talk about how we can use words from the prophet and apostles as "modern scriptures" in our lives. You could also offer a mini-lesson where highlights from that month's church magazines are shared.

"PJ'S PARTY"

Have sisters wear modest pajamas and bring stuffed animals, pillows, blankets, and bed-time accessories. Eat late-night snacks, do each other's hair, talk about boys (ways to spice up marriage), and then talk about another meaning for PJ's: Prayer, Journal, and Scriptures. Award prizes to everyone who dresses up for the most creative pajamas.

"AND IT CAME TO PASS"

Form a study group for sisters who would like to meet frequently and study a certain book of scripture or topics. Have them report to all of the sisters on some insights that were gained during their time together. Talk to your Bishop or Stake President about creating a special adult's Institute class in your area.

"ARTICLES OF FAITH BAR"

Have a lesson about how the Articles of Faith were created and share ideas on how sisters can help their families memorize them. For dessert that evening you could have an "Articles of Faith Bar" where each Article of Faith represents a different item such as a spoon, bowl, napkin, ice cream scoop, and different toppings. When the sisters recite an Article of Faith they receive each of the corresponding items.

"MARY AND MARTHA"

Discuss the women that are mentioned in the scriptures and the roles they played. Talk about what lessons can be learned from them and how the Lord sees women in His kingdom today.

SABBATH DAY OBSERVANCE

"SABBATH STATIONS"

Show sisters how to make a Sunday activity box or create "Sabbath Stations" for the family to rotate through at home after church that include activities appropriate for Sunday, such as writing letters to missionaries and relatives, journal writing, playing hymns on an instrument they're learning, watching a Church video, listening to scriptures on tape, etc.

"SUPER SUNDAYS"

There's a terrific book entitled *Sabbath Solutions* (shameless plug) that sisters could discuss to brainstorm ways they can keep the Sabbath Day holy and make their Sunday worship more meaningful. The book includes ideas for all ages, from young children all the way up to older adults who are "young at heart." It also discusses the history of the Sabbath and how the Lord uses it as a sign and covenant with his people. Serve ice cream "Sundays," of course!

"BLOOMING INSPIRATIONS" OR "FOR THE BEAUTY OF THE EARTH"

Teach the ladies how to make beautiful floral arrangements to decorate the chapel and other areas of the church on Sundays and special events.

"HEALING HYMNALS"

Spend some time repairing the hymnals in your church building. Talk about the importance of caring for the facilities and the importance of music. Play beautiful hymns while sisters tape and glue book bindings, unfold dog-eared pages, and erase markings that little children's hands have made on the hymn books.

Discuss the history of the first hymn book Emma Smith was asked to create for the early Saints. Have someone perform some favorite hymns.

"BLESSED BREAD"

This class will teach sisters how to make bread that could be used for the Sacrament (and their families.) Have sisters sign up on a calendar to take turns supplying the bread each Sunday for your ward.

"HIDDEN GEMS"

Take the sisters on a tour of the library in your church building and have them discover some of the hidden gems inside. Invite the ward librarian to show them all of the resources that are available for them to take home and enjoy on Sundays (and any day of the week), such as church videos, flannel board stories to borrow for Family Home Evening, church books, and resources for preparing talks or lessons. If your librarian needs help, your "tour" could include some time creating an inventory, cleaning shelves and counters, or preparing picture packets for teachers to use on Sunday.

"PUBLIC SPEAKING 101" OR "EXTRAORDINARY TALKS BY ORDINARY PEOPLE"

Invite a leader from your local Toastmasters Club to share tips on public speaking. Discuss formulas for writing a good Sacrament meeting talk and how to overcome the fear of speaking in front of people in a formal setting. Everyone is nervous about standing in front of a congregation to speak, but I have yet to see anyone ever pass out. Well, there was that one time . . .

Have sisters practice good form and replace fidgets and bad habits with confidence. If you have tough sisters who can handle it, you could even video the sisters as they make a short presentation to show them how they look when they speak. Offer SENSITIVE, helpful ideas on how they could improve.

"NATURE WALKS"

Have someone tell the sisters about peaceful locations around your town where they and their families could go on Sundays to reflect. Talk about places where they could go for nature walks and make Nature Journals where they could write down their thoughts and glue things they find that inspire them, such as leaves and flowers. Read poems by David Thoreau and other writers who felt the presence of God in nature.

"THE SMALL PLATES"

Nephi kept historical records on "large plates" and wrote about more spiritual matters on "small plates." Have the sisters create Spiritual Journals where they record their testimonies and spiritual experiences. Use a new craft style or technique that the sisters would like to learn to design their books or binders.

CHAPTER FIVE

Homemaking Skills

Proverbs 31:27 "She looketh well to the ways of her household, and eateth not the bread of idleness."

GROWING FOOD

"SECRET GARDEN"

Have a lesson on container gardening and how to plant food in small spaces for apartment dwellers and sisters with very small backyards. Show sisters how to plant in strawberry pots, use mini tomato cages, and attach wire to exterior walls for vines to climb on. Have each sister take home a small potted herb plant to start growing on her kitchen window-sill. Show the sisters that we can all follow the prophet's counsel to plant a garden, even in the smallest of spaces!

"HOE HOE HOE" OR "GREEN THUMB TRAINING"

Invite a speaker from a local plant nursery to share planting tips and show various types of plants that are popular and easy to grow. He could even show unusual plants and how to care for them. Give plants as door prizes for sisters who arrive at Enrichment Night on time, carpool or bring a friend. Talk about the differences between annuals and perennials. Read President Kimball's counsel to the Saints to beautify our homes and yards.

"GARDENING FOR DUMMIES"

Have your resident green thumb expert share gardening tips. Talk about successful methods for planting fruit trees, a vegetable garden, rose garden, landscaping, etc. Call your county Extension service to find a Master Gardener in your area who could share his/her knowledge. The Extension office has pamphlets and great information on everything from lawn care to canning peaches! They can also provide you with kits to determine what your soil content is.

"MEET HERB" OR " THE HERBAL HARVEST"

Teach sisters all about growing and cooking different kinds of herbs. Share ideas and designs for planting a traditional English herb garden, pizza topping garden (tomatoes, basil, onions, garlic, etc), salad bowl garden, and other clever combinations. Talk about why home grown herbs are more economical and flavorful.

"WILD THING"

Learn about local and wild plants that are unique to your area. Talk about native grasses and discuss which plants are invasive to your garden and which ones are worth keeping around. Learn how to make baskets or wreaths out of native vines. Someone from your local botanical garden could share information and bring samples.

"THIS AIN'T NO BRUSSELS SPROUT" OR "SPROUT SISTERS"

Learn how to sprout different kinds of legumes (lentils, mung, azuki, chick peas), grassy seeds (alfalfa, mustard, sesame), or grains (barley, oats, wheat). Learn how to use them in soups, salads or sandwiches. Have a contest to see who could guess where different sprouts came from. Discuss how to store them with your other food storage items.

"H_2O FLOW"

Learn how to garden using less water. Discuss xeroscaping, hydroscaping and other popular water conservation techniques such as drip irrigation and soaker hoses. Show different kinds of cacti and other drought tolerant plant material. Invite someone from your local Water Department to share other water conservation efforts the sisters can do in their home. Invite a water bottling company to explain how that process works. Discuss how to store water for emergencies and how to keep your water storage clean of contaminants.

"STOP BUGGING ME"

Learn which pesticides and weed controls are better for your area. Discuss natural and safer alternatives to treating garden problems. Share ideas about how to decrease the mosquito population in your yard for outside parties and BBQs. Show pictures of common garden bugs so sisters can know what to recognize. This class is not for the squeamish! Discuss how to protect your family from the West Nile virus.

"FARMER'S MARKET"

Learn when to harvest fruit, veggies and berries and learn their shelf life. Discuss how to pick out fresh fruits and vegetables when you're buying them from the store or fruit stand at the side of the road. Talk about how to keep produce crisp in the refrigerator and how to speed up ripeness by using a brown paper bag. Talk about how to include the freshest edibles in your food storage.

"GARDENING ANGEL" OR "AGRICULTURAL HALL"

Compare tips on getting rid of rodents and plant-killing animals in your yard. Talk about deer-resistant landscape and which household tales are true and which ones aren't. For example, does it really work to put human hair from your brush in old hosiery and hang them from trees to keep deer away? Share stories about what our pioneer ancestors did.

"VEGGIE SWAP"

At the end of the summer when people are drowning in garden-grown tomatoes and zucchini have the sisters do a "Veggie Swap" where they can exchange their garden crops for others' produce. Award blue ribbons for the best produce. Have sisters share tips on how they grew their produce.

"PUMPKIN PATCH"

This is a fun class to offer in October to teach the sisters how to carve their Jack-O-Lantern, how to grow pumpkins, how to decorate their home and holiday table with different kinds of squash and gourds, how to cook pumpkin seeds and make pumpkin desserts.

"HERE WE GROW AGAIN"

Teach the sisters how to propagate and share plant clippings with one another. You could provide a plant exchange. Teach how to care for seedlings. Show how to divide tubor plants such as Day Lilies, Hosta, and other perennials.

"DO EAT THE DAISIES"

This ain't your grandma's garnish! For an unusual class, discuss cooking with edible flowers and share recipes for salads, soups, drinks, and even desserts. Be sure to teach the sisters about which flowers NOT to eat and other how to identify poisonous plants. You could also combine all of this information with a lesson in flower arranging. Talk about some of the wild plants our pioneer ancestors ate along the trail.

"WASTE NOT WANT NOT" OR "GOLD DIRT"

Teach the sisters all about composting, organic gardening, and different kinds of mulch for the garden. Introduce different kinds of compost bins from store bought to home-made.

COOKING FOOD

"A MUCH KNEADED CLASS" OR "KNEAD TO KNOW BASICS"

Here's a good old homemaking classic: learn how to make homemade breads & rolls. Learn how to shape and twist dough to create unique loaves. Discuss the differences between hard winter wheat, soft white wheat, Baker's bread flour, etc. Learn how to bake bread to use for the Sacrament and create a sign-up list so sisters can take turns providing it each Sunday.

"ONE DISH WONDERS"

Offer a class about crock-pot cooking. Share entrée recipes that could be started right before leaving for church and that would be ready to eat when the family returns a few hours later. There are even breakfast recipes that cook overnight and provide early risers (those Seminary kids, for example) a hot, quick breakfast.

"TALK THE WOK"

Have someone teach a class on how to use a wok for cooking Chinese food, low fat dishes, and healthy stir-fries. You could even combine the class with a lesson about Chinese culture. Teach the sisters how to season a wok and properly care for it in between uses. Share new ways to cook all those vegetables from our gardens.

"EAT YOUR WHEATIES" OR
"IF YE ARE PREPARED YE SHALL NOT FEAR"

Learn how to use your food storage in every day cooking. Have a Taster's Table using dishes with wheat, legumes, dried milk and other items that we often buy for our storage but don't quite know how to use!

"DEHYDRATED WATER AND MORE!"

Teach the sisters how to bake, using dehydrated products such as powdered milk, dehydrated butter flakes, powdered eggs and cheese, etc. Have sisters share their success stories using food storage items in their baking. Taste everything!

"WHEN LIFE GIVES YOU LEMONS"

Make different kinds of things with lemons such as lemonade, lemon squares, lemon merengue pie, lemon poppy seed muffins, lemon zest, and more! In addition to all of the fun cooking you could carry the theme further into other "lemony" classes such as having a positive attitude, how to make your own lemon scented home fresheners or furniture polish, and cute craft projects like hand- painted lemonade pitchers and glasses.

"BETTER THAN BUNS OF STEEL"

Learn how to make specialty breads such as sourdough, scones, pita bread, friendship bread, quick breads, etc. Have everyone take home a sourdough starter or one of those Amish friendship bread mixtures to start with their friends.

"I CAN'T BELIEVE IT'S BUTTER!"

Teach the sisters how to make their own butter, cooking sprays and margarine using canola oil and butter products to create a more healthy and economical version. Sample different kinds. Discuss fats in foods and share light recipes. Learn how to make cute butter pads using molds of different shapes and sizes to add more flair to the dinner table and for special events.

"IT'S A WRAP!"

This class is all about cooking with tortillas, gyros, lettuce wraps, pita pockets, cabbage rolls and breadless sandwiches for low carbohydrate meals. Share creative ideas for kids' lunches and how to disguise healthy foods in kids' snacks.

"SAY CHEESE!"

Have someone teach the sisters how to make their own cheese, yogurt and other dairy products. Offer samples of different kinds of cheeses that are really popular right now such as goat cheese, Gorgonzala, herbed Feta, baked Brie and more. Show how to use dehydrated milk from your food storage to create less expensive versions of your favorite dairy products. Share recipes and taste everything!

"FUNERAL POTATOES AND MORE"

Have a sister or even a panel of sisters share recipes and cooking tips for making The perfect "Mormon" casserole. Share tips on great meals to take to moms with newborn babies, or when another sister is sick or someone is in the hospital. Talk about which meals freeze well to give to families when Mom isn't able to cook.

"THERE'S ALWAYS ROOM FOR JELL-O"

You could hold a contest to see how creative sisters can be with gelatin to combat the reputation we Relief Society sisters have of serving only boring, green Jell-o at every dinner! Use cute molds to create interesting shapes and teach sisters how to make layered gelatin dishes. Share recipes kids can use to make fun, jiggly treats. Write a letter to Bill Cosby. (just kidding)

"THE GIFT OF GOOD TASTE"

This would be a fun class full of ideas of things you could make and bake from your kitchen to give as gifts, especially at Christmas time. Items could include cookie kits, biscuit mixes, applesauce ornaments, brownie mixes, pancake mixes, etc. Gifts could even be assembled to give away as Visiting Teaching treats or put in care packages to missionaries, college students or military servicemen. Sisters could decorate bags, jars, and labels to package their gifts. You could also sew cute drawstring pouches for rice or bean mixes. Include a plastic liner if the mix contains powder.

"PASS OVER THE MATZAH!"

Learn about foods used during the Passover. It would be so interesting to invite a Jewish friend to share some of the food traditions she has enjoyed in her family. Learn about the symbolism and discuss Passover in Old and New Testament scriptures. Taste samples and learn about how food is prepared in order to be considered Kosher. Invite women from a local Jewish group to teach you how to prepare traditional Jewish foods.

"CHRISTMAS COOKIE CLUB"

A fun class would be to share all kinds of recipes for Christmas cookies. This would be a great Taster's Table idea as well. If sisters are interested they could form a Christmas Cookie Club where they would each bake a certain amount of cookies and then exchange them with each other so that they all went home with a variety of cookies for the holidays. Find "gospel-oriented" cookie cutters or design your own.

"WHO YOU CALLING TURKEY?"

Have one of your older, experienced sisters share her cooking successes over the years preparing Thanksgiving dinners. It would also be fun to have a creative sister share unusual Thanksgiving alternatives for people with diabetes or nut allergies, vegetarians or people on low-carb diets. Create a Thanksgiving cookbook or share recipes for cooking the perfect bird and all the trimmings. You could also offer classes where sisters could make Thanksgiving table linens, talk about holiday traditions, create Family Home Evening packets so children learn the story of the First Thanksgiving, and how to make creative, yet inexpensive napkin rings and place settings.

"SUMMER SALADS" OR "SCENTSATIONAL SUMMER"

This could be a class showcasing different kinds of salads, a Taster's Table, or the title of a summer potluck picnic. Show creative ways to dress up salads and toss interesting things into them like Jicama, dried cranberries, glazed nuts, orange zest, etc. Give prizes for the most unusual salad, yummiest, fanciest, best dressed, etc. Discuss the Word of Wisdom. Be sure to share recipes!

"SWEET AS PIE"

Surely there is a sister in your ward who is well known for making the most scrumptious pies. Reveal secrets for making the best pie crust and show different kinds of pies using one crust and two. Share tips and include a variety of pies such as baked pies, meat pies, empanadas, Shepherd's pie, and refrigerator cream pies. Mmmm. You could use a Greek theme and initiate sisters into the "I Eta Pi" Club on your Relief Society "campus."

"RICE TO THE OCCASION"

This class is everything you wanted to know about rice but were afraid to ask. Sample different kinds of rice such as pilaf, brown, steamed, fried, and wild. Show how to use rice as a crust in casseroles, different ways to wrap rice for weddings, use it to make mosaic art projects, and rice mixes as gifts. Talk about how to prepare rice for your food storage.

"YOU TAKE THE CAKE!"

Offer a class on how to decorate cakes for special events. If no one in your ward knows how, you could always invite someone from the bakery department of a local store or pastry shop to show you how. Have sisters practice on cupcakes or each woman could bring a cake to decorate that she could then take home to share with her own family. Prepare another cake for all of the sisters to eat that night or to present to sisters who are celebrating birthdays that month. Share ideas for fun cake traditions to start in your family and the importance of creating "sweet" memories.

"JUST A LITTLE ON THE TOP"

Sisters could learn how to decorate sugar cookies for various occasions (Christmas, Valentine's Day, Easter, birthdays, etc). I know, it's not hard to slap frosting on a cookie . . . think Martha Stewart. Learn how to create elegant designs and try using different kinds of edible decorations. You could hold a cookie decorating contest or simply let the sisters decorate cookies to take home for each person in their family or as refreshments for all of the sisters that night. Show examples of how to dip cookies in chocolate, make cookie sandwiches, or even gingerbread houses and men (and women). Offer tips on how to carefully transport edible treasures to potlucks, school functions or to other events.

"THE MELTING POT"

Teach sisters how to create meals and desserts using a fondue pot. Have them sample different kinds of fondue, such as cheese, white and dark chocolates, hot oils, broth, etc. Try dipping all kinds of things from fruits, vegetables, crusty breads to meats, cheeses, candy and nuts. You could also show how to prepare simple foods on camping stoves, with Sterno, or other equipment when the power goes out in your house!

"GRANDMA'S GRITS AND GRUB"

Gather the sisters' favorite family recipes and create a ward cookbook. This would make a great gift to the sisters at Christmas time or for the Relief Society birthday in March. Have sisters contribute their favorite recipe in categories such as entrée's with meat, chicken dishes, crock-pot meals, desserts, salads, soups, breads, breakfast when company is in town, quick breakfasts for Seminary students, hors d'eourves, beverages, veggies, etc. Share a copy of your cookbook with your Stake Relief Society presidency!

"PATRIOTIC PICNIC"

This can be held outside on the grass as a basket dinner, indoors with tables decorated with red checkered fabric and plastic ants, or as a class full of ideas on packing a great picnic meal for the family. You could offer another class where sisters could build small picnic tables for their toddlers using wood pieces cut out ahead of time. If you use a patriotic theme you could sing the theme songs of each branch of the military, read quotes from famous Americans, sing patriotic songs, make flag pins and other patriotic clothing and home décor. Pass out patriotic stationery so the sisters can write letters to our servicemen (and women) stationed overseas.

"HOSTESS WITH THE MOSTEST"

This class would teach the sisters how to host a buffet dinner with many guests. Demonstrate creative table decorations and food display tips. Show how to use different sized objects under tablecloths to create lifts and levels for a professional effect. Have sisters learn how to make those fancy radish flowers and other veggies, using various kitchen tools. Encourage sisters to reach out to their neighbors by inviting them over! Talk about great neighborhood traditions your family could start where you live.

"WHERE'S THE BEEF?" OR "THIS COW IS MAD"

Learn about all of the different cuts of beef there are and how to make the best selection for your recipes. Invite a butcher to talk about marbleized beef, grain fed cows, veal, expiration dates, freezing tips, etc. Decorate with a cow motif. Talk about the role of meat in the Word of Wisdom.

"OLD FASHIONED COUNTRY FAIR"

Decorate with lots of gingham fabrics and raffia. Have sisters bring various dishes to be judged for blue ribbon prizes. Encourage the ladies to display their handicraft items and learn how to do country crafts like tole painting. It would be great to offer information and discount coupons for any county fairs going on in your area. Scatter stuffed animal pigs and cows for the obligatory livestock booths at the fair. Discuss good ole pioneer heritage and handicraft.

"BERRY INTERESTING"

This class would teach sisters how to grow, cook and preserve different kinds of berries. Share ideas for making cobblers, jams, sauces, fruit leather, and more!

"SOUP'S ON!"

This could be a class full of ideas and recipes, a Taster's Table, or an entire meal served for the evening, when combined with yummy rolls and breads. Show sisters how to get creative with different kinds of soup toppings and teach them how to make their own tortilla strips, oyster crackers, or grilled veggie mix-ins. Decorate using aprons and those old fashioned, red Campbell soup labels. Talk about how to sneak healthy grains and veggies into soups and other foods your family eats.

"GREAT GRAINS"

We all know about wheat and probably have hundreds of pounds of it stored somewhere around our house, but there are soooo many other grains we could be using too! Teach sisters about kamut, teff, amaranth, flax, quinoa, hemp, faro and more, many of which have tons of protein in them! Talk about how to combine grains and legumes to form a complete protein. Check out www.chefbrad.com. (Every year he cooks dinner for his former mission president and one of his companions, so maybe he'll cook me dinner if I mention him in this book.) Learn how to camouflage grains in other foods to stretch your food dollar and make meals more healthy.

"SMOOTH AS ICE"

Set up your own juice bar and show sisters how to make blended drinks, Slurpies, Icees, Piña Coladas, and Daqueris (all virgin, of course). Talk about other non-alcoholic beverages that could be served at parties, New Year's Eve, and other special occasions. Talk about juicing machines and how to get those "5 A Day" fruits and veggies into our meals.

"BAAAM!"

Invite a professional chef to share gourmet cooking tips and how to make a fancy presentation of even the most simple meal. Make the sisters feel like they're really in Culinary school by creating chef hats for everyone to wear. Teach sisters how to chop veggies like the masters and do those cool swirly designs on dessert plates with different fruit, cream, and chocolate sauces. Talk about the importance of eating together as a family during meal time and how to create fond food memories.

"BON APPETITE"

The Bon Appetite cooking magazine has a section where readers ask the Editor to convince restaurants to share recipes for some of their most popular items. Everyone wants to know how to make those yummy Mrs. Fields Chocolate Chip cookies, Red Lobster biscuits, or TGI Friday's Potato Skins for example! Share recipes for "mock" versions of some of those favorites. This class could also teach how to make less expensive versions of store bought goodies like Oreo cookies, Bisquick mix, graham crackers and more.

"UNDER THE SEA"

This could be a class or an entire Relief Society dinner. Decorate tables with sea shells and ocean motif. Learn how to cook seafood. Some sisters may have never tasted clams, squid, mussels, scallops, shark, etc. Ask a local seafood restaurant to donate discount coupons or samples.

"IN THE LINE OF FIRE"

It probably won't be hard to find one of the men in your ward who wants to show off his BBQ skills. Show sisters how to grill different kinds of meat, chicken, fish, veggies, fruit and bread. Talk about what to look for when buying a grill and how to keep it clean in the summer and stored properly during the winter. Sisters could make and decorate BBQ aprons for themselves or their husbands.

"TASTE OF HOME"

Have your resident party queen share tips on how to host formal and casual dinner parties. Give ideas on how to fellowship other families in your ward, create catchy invitations, plan a neighborhood Block Party, host a Friday Game Night with friends, and serve cook-ahead meals that allow the hostess to enjoy her guests instead of slaving away in the kitchen.

"EPICURIOUS"

Offer a class that teaches women how to properly sharpen their kitchen knives and shears, and care for their cooking utensils. Demonstrate fun kitchen gadgets. Have a contest to see who could invent the most unique tool. Talk about creative ways to decorate the kitchen and dining areas. Show pictures of unique kitchen designs and offer ideas on how the sisters could incorporate commercial kitchen ware into their own homes. If you get really ambitious you could have sisters make hanging pot racks out of wood, medal or other materials. Ask a Tupperware sales person to donate a few containers as door prizes. Give sisters practical ideas on how to store all their kitchen stuff!

"DEATH BY CHOCOLATE"

What female wouldn't want to attend a class with a title like that? Besides showing all kinds of ways to cook with chocolate, the teacher of this class could explain the emotional and physiological connection women have with chocolate. You could also open up the class to a variety of decadent desserts, not just chocolate ones. Did you know a favorite chicken dish of Mexico called Mole' has chocolate as one of its ingredients? I suppose a little lesson about "moderation in all things" would be a gentle reminder to not overdo it with chocolate . . .

"THE APRICOT TREE"

Learn everything you can do with popcorn! Sing the famous Primary song or invite some children to share a musical number for that old Primary favorite. Make popcorn balls, show different things to add to your Christmas popcorn strings and share recipes for making different blends such as parmesan garlic, peanut butter, caramel, etc. You could even talk about different kinds of packing peanuts! Did you know that your kids could build things out of the biodegradable packing peanuts made with a corn starch base? All they have to do is lick the ends and they'll stick together! I wouldn't recommend eating their masterpiece, however. How many of you have popcorn in your food storage?

PRESERVING FOOD

"MANNA FROM HEAVEN"

Learn how to make dehydrated foods like beef jerky, onion bits, bacon bits, croutons, fruit leather, etc. Discuss different kinds of dehydrating machines and even how to use a microwave or oven to achieve a similar product. Show how to add dried foods to your home storage.

"EXTREME HOME STORAGE MAKEOVER"

This is a great project to have the Elders Quorum help with! Build food storage rotating shelves out of wood, wire racks, or shelving on wheels. Show pictures of other kinds of rotating systems. Show different ways to keep an inventory of food storage items and how to rotate them into your every day cooking.

"EARTH ELEMENTS"

Make potpourri from dried flowers, pinecones and other backyard items. Wrap them as gifts. Decorate special bags or boxes. You could also sew tie-string bags to put the contents in. Learn about scented oils that could be sprinkled on potpourri mixers to freshen them up. Talk about other ways to create pleasant smells in our homes and how to get rid of the yucky ones!

"THE FRUITS OF YOUR LABOR"

Show sisters how to make jams and jellies. Teach how to choose the right kind of fruit for canning. A fun Taster's Table would be filled with different kinds of rolls, muffins, toast, and bread to sample all the flavors of jellies and jams. Show other kinds of jams like jalapeño jelly over cream cheese served with crackers, or mint jelly that compliments roast lamb. Decorate jars with home-made labels and cute lids with fabric or clay designs. Talk about how to grow fruit in our gardens and include it in our food storage plan.

"BEAUTIFUL BOTTLES"

Learn how to make decorative vinegar bottles and herb or spice-infused oils as gifts and for cooking. Show samples of bottles with herbs, garlic, peppers, lemons, oranges, bay leaves, mint, etc. Wrap bottles with raffia and make pretty labels. Talk about cooking with herbs and fresh spices.

"FOILED AGAIN!"

This class teaches the ladies how to keep vegetables, fruit, cheese, dairy, and leftovers fresh in the refrigerator. Demonstrate different kinds of containers and wraps. Talk about how long certain foods are still safe to eat once you've taken them out of the fridge and what the shelf life is for certain products. Your County Extension office will have pamphlets for common guidelines for freezing and storing food in your climate. You could also talk about how to store different foods and prepared meals in the freezer.

"MEALS IN MINUTES"

Learn how to cut your cooking time by using the now famous system for making thirty days worth of meals in one day and freezing them for later use throughout the month. Talk about how to freeze food flat to make more room in the freezer. Discuss which foods should never be stored together and how long foods can be left in the freezer without losing nutritional value and flavor. Be sure to give tips on how to prevent freezer burn. You could also turn this into a big service project event by helping a soon-to-be mom cook up some meals in advance so that when her baby arrives she'll only have to thaw and heat and then get on to more important things like snuggling with that new, little one!

"HOME-MADE PRESERVES"

You could plan an entire evening with this theme, offering classes in how to preserve food, family heirlooms, photos, food storage, and memories, etc.

HOME ORGANIZATION AND CLEANING

"MORMON MAKEOVER"

Find a creative sister to teach a class on how to tastefully display gospel beliefs in the home by using pictures of temples and prophets, family tree décor, wall hangings, handicraft, pioneer heirlooms, church awards, replicas of church sculptures, etc. Talk about how, without looking like frumpy Mormon clutter, we can use our house as a missionary tool that reflects our religious values.

"ELBOW GREASE"

Every sister who has struggled with common household stains would like this class! Talk about how to get rid of common (and not so common) laundry stains, carpet odors and messes, spots on upholstery, how to repair auto interiors and even knicked furniture.

"ENLIGHTENMENT"

Teach sisters how to properly clean the windows in her home, including window frames and blinds. Discuss different kinds of window treatments (shutters, blinds, Roman shades, valances, cornice boxes, etc.) and how to care for them as well. Show creative window treatments using unique items for hardware to create a thematic design in the room, such as golf clubs, shutters, flower boxes, fishing rods, tree branches, etc. (Okay, maybe that sounds weird, but it's all the rage with interior decorators these days!)

"MISS ORDERLY CONDUCT"

This class is to help moms know how to organize their children's rooms, school papers, sports equipment and game schedules, music lesson information, stuffed animal collection, and all the other clutter that often surrounds children. Discuss how to motivate children to want to be organized themselves. Create charts and offer ideas for different kinds of incentive programs that could be used.

"HOME MATTERS"

For sisters living in colder climates you could offer a class on how to clean and ready their furnace for winter. Other winterizing tips could be discussed for autos, outdoor summer furniture, clothing, summer toys, BBQs, weatherizing, and the proper care of other seasonal items for the home.

"CARPET CARE" OR "SWEPT UNDER THE RUG"

Offer a lesson in how to properly clean and maintain the carpets and upholstery in your home. Compare different methods (steam, chem-dry, foam) and talk about different kinds of carpets and how various products respond to them. Ask one of your local home improvement stores or carpet cleaning companies to offer discount coupons to class participants or to lead the discussion. It would also be a good time to talk about common allergens in the home and helpful remedies.

"QUEEN OF CLEAN"

Learn how to clean anything! There are plenty of good products out there to help with the job, but you could also learn how to make less expensive, homemade alternatives. Share tips, and success stories as well as cleaning failures. Be sure to talk about toxic combinations of cleansers and cleaning solutions so the sisters will know how to keep their homes safe. Mention child-safety latches on cleaning cabinets and offer ideas on how to keep children and pets safe from harmful products.

"CLUTTER'S LAST STAND"

Learn how to de-clutter our homes and our lives. Offer tips on organizing garages, home office, those kitchen junk drawers, and other common spots where clutter accumulates in our homes. Share ideas on how to eliminate unnecessary clutter from our lives and how to prioritize. Share tips on how to prepare for a garage sale.

"MAKE A SPLASH WITH SOAP" OR "SPLISH SPLASH"

Make decorative soaps, bath bubbles, and bath salts. Who says getting clean has to be dirty work? These would make great gifts for Mother's Day, Visiting Teaching, Relief Society birthday or Christmas. To add a spiritual dimension to this class you could have someone teach a mini-lesson on repentance and the importance of being spiritually clean.

"SILKS ALIVE"

Learn how to clean silk plants, dried flowers, topiaries, and other artificial plants and trees that often attract so much dust. You could even learn how to create lovely displays for the home or even to decorate the Relief Society room, chapel, or other areas of your church building. Offer to make one for the Young Women's room that you can change the colored flowers in each month to coordinate with their rotating value colors and theme!

"MR. CLEAN" OR "WASH DAY SECRETS REVEALED"

Share laundry and ironing tips. Would you believe there are actually tons of web sites that offer tips for this kind of stuff? This would be a fun class to invite the sisters' sons to as a missionary preparation skill! You could even practice sewing on buttons, repairing zippers, attaching Velcro or snaps to fabric, hemming pants, etc. This class should attract the moms who want to know how to get the stink and stains out of all the clothes that the men in their life accumulate.

"WELCOME HOME"

Learn how to make your home smell sweet with scented oils for lamps, linen water, scented sprays, potpourri, candles, incense, cooking, scented bags in the clothes dryer, and more. Sisters could learn how to make and use various items. Invite the owner of a local candle store to share samples and talk about the care of candles and fire safety.

"CURB APPEAL"

Learn about the first impression your house makes and how to improve that message. Invite a Realtor to share ideas on how to make your house more appealing from the front exterior. Talk about landscaping, front door care, architectural improvements, exterior paint, driveway and concrete materials, lighting, and yard clutter.

"LET YOUR LIGHT SO SHINE"

Have the sisters learn about different kinds of lighting for their home to bring out the colors in your home, save energy costs, and decorate for form and function. Discuss different kinds of lighting fixtures, including track lights, sconces, chandeliers, pendants, ceiling fans, up-lights, spotlights, can lights, florescent, task lighting, accents and more. Sister could also learn how to make different kinds of candles for their home and to give as gifts.

"IF WALLS COULD TALK"

Show sisters proper patching and painting techniques for painting the interior and exterior walls in their home. Discuss lead in paint, varnishes, faux finishes, wood stains, how to use painter's tape, and other applications.

"WILD ABOUT WALLPAPER"

Have sisters learn how to hang wallpaper and borders, as well as use wallpaper to decorate shelving, furniture, window treatments, ceilings, for wrapping presents and more! Most wallpaper stores will give you their old wallpaper sample books to use for crafts or other things.

"GREEN CARPET"

Teach sisters how to mow and edge the lawn correctly, how to select the right lawnmower, recommendations for lawn restoration and choosing grasses, lawn disease, maintenance, hiring a gardener, and other yard work tips.

"FIX IT UP" OR "WOOD YOU LIKE TO KNOW?"

Learn how to refinish old furniture to make pieces last longer and restore them to a thing of beauty. Talk about stripping paint, sanding, stains, upholstery, shellacs and varnish, and how to repair damages.

"ANOTHER MAN'S TREASURE"

Learn the ins and outs of having a garage sale to get rid of all that junk once and for all! Talk about how to prepare, price and display items. Any sisters who want to get rid of their junk NOW could bring it to Enrichment Night and you could have a mini-garage sale or "Give Away" night.

THE VALUE OF WORK

"ROUND TUITS" OR "PROCRASTINATOR'S PROJECTS"

Help sisters learn how to prioritize household tasks and overcome procrastination. Have sisters decorate a wide-mouthed jar. Provide slips of paper and pencils where they will write down all of the jobs they keep putting off. Encourage the sisters to draw out an assignment once a week and accomplish that task. Give awards for the most creative excuses for procrastinating. Discuss the importance of not being idle and how to get motivated to work.

"FLOWERS IN A BOX"

This class teaches how to design and plant pretty flower boxes for every season. Talk about amendments that could be added to the soil to improve hydration, plants that grow best in sun and shade, mounting boxes to different exterior surfaces, combining flowers that cascade with upright growth, and attractive color combinations. You could even have sisters build a flower box for their home. Show sisters how all of their hard work will be richly rewarded each season.

"EVERYTHING'S COMING UP ROSES"

This class discusses how to care for rose bushes in the yard as well as rose bouquets in vases, how to dry flowers for decorating your home and making gifts. Show different varieties of roses and introduce the sisters to some of the hybrids created and named for celebrities. Learn how to make those cute roses using Hershey kisses, floral tape and cellophane. I put this class under the "value of work" category because most people think growing roses is a lot of work, but it's not if you know how to do it the right way!

"HONEY DO"

This class addresses such issues as the division of labor in your home, chore charts, task reminders you can use on your computer or calendar, suggested guidelines for routine maintenance, and how to get motivated to crack that list of things to be done! Talk about what work needs to be done to beautify your home and yard. Single sisters could also be taught how to repair basic items when they don't have a "honey" around to help them.

"PIONEER PICNIC"

Have a pioneer meal and talk about all of the hard work our pioneer ancestors had to do each day. Sing pioneer songs and share inspiring stories. Put cream in baby food jars to shake while you're telling stories and watch it turn into butter. Cook pioneer biscuits over a fire by wrapping dough around a wood block soaked in water that is attached to a metal rod or stick. Teach sisters how to do Dutch Oven cooking or sew pioneer bonnets for their daughters. For cheap entertainment, attach those plastic surgical gloves to a cardboard cow for sisters to pretend to milk.

"THE HAPPY HOMEMAKER"

Discuss the joys of homemaking and the value of hard work. Help sisters remember that the work they do within the walls of their home is not only important, but also sacred. Talk about how to find happiness and joy in every day living.

"A WOMAN'S WORK" OR "BRINGING HOME THE BACON"

Offer a class for women in the workplace to find balance in their lives. Help them feel supported in their efforts, especially if they are single moms trying to do it all. Talk about helpful resources in and out of the church, job burnout, and the importance of time management and health.

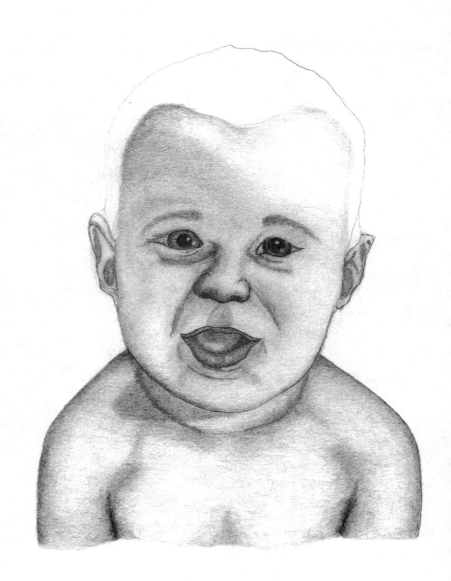

CHAPTER SIX

Marriage and Family Relations

Mosiah 4:15 "But ye will teach them to walk in the ways of truth and soberness; ye will teach them to love one another, and to serve one another."

Malachi 4:6 "And he shall turn the heart of the fathers to the children, and the heart of the children to their fathers, lest I come and smite the earth with a curse."

THE FAMILY: A PROCLAMATION TO THE WORLD

"HOMESPUN HAPPINESS"

This class could involve a sewing or craft project such as making frames or wall hangings to display "The Family: A Proclamation To The World."

Another class could be a presentation about what the Proclamation means and how we can stand for righteousness and truth in our community. You can also print the Proclamation on vellum and place it over a picture of your family or Christ.

"BEYOND HARLEQUIN" OR "AFTER THE HONEYMOON"

Find a creative teacher to share ideas on how to keep the romance in your marriage. The class could also be taught by an experienced husband, a married couple or even a panel of selected people (preferably happily married ones!) There are some great ideas to be found at www.lovingyou.com, www.beromanantic.com, and www.theromantic.com.

"TURNING THE HEARTS"

This class is about, of course, Family History. You could have a heart-themed evening with cute heart decorations, heart-shaped food, and even a heart crafts project or two. The class could be held inside your family history library for a real hands-on approach if you're fortunate enough to have one in your building. Teach sisters how to get started with their own family history and talk about all of the Internet resources that are now available.

"FOCUS ON THE FAMILY"

Share great ideas for family photos for Christmas or any other time of year. Show sisters how to create a photo pedigree display for their walls or to keep with their Book of Remembrance. Invite a photographer to share tips on taking good pictures, what colors work best, and different backgrounds that create appeal and interest. Talk about the do's and don'ts of taking a good picture. Discuss different kinds of cameras, film, and photograph paper. Have one of the scrapbooking queens in your ward (I know you have one) to show ideas for great pictures and photo albums.

"BEYOND THE PEDIGREE CHART"

This class could be about more advanced genealogy techniques or even have a completely different twist to Family History, that of writing personal histories and autobiographies. Share examples of different kinds of biographies and provide a list or cute jar of "writer's block starters" to give sisters ideas of what to write about in their autobiographies. Invite someone from your local genealogy chapter to share ideas and stories.

"WHISPERS FROM BEYOND THE VEIL"

There are tons of books and even a PBS TV series that share amazing and inspiring stories of regular folks trying to research their family's roots. Share inspiring stories that help sisters to know that while we are reaching beyond the veil that the Lord is there to help. You could even collect stories from your ward members to put into a special book to give as a gift to all the sisters, to your Bishopric, to missionaries serving from your ward or share in a ward newsletter. Learn how to effectively write true genealogy stories.

"FAMILY MATTERS"

Teach sisters how to create a family motto, family mission statement, family song or even a family flag. Talk about how to research your family's coat of arms or how to design a new one. Teach sisters how to display these things in different forms such as wall hangings, plaques, cross-stitch pillows or pictures in frames, painted on walls, etc. Share ideas on how to get children interested in learning about their ancestors.

"OPEN ARMS"

Information from this class should be handled with great sensitivity. Invite someone from the LDS Social Services or a couple who has gone through this process to share their feelings and experiences about adoption, infertility, and foster care parenting.

"CELEBRATING YOUR ROOTS" OR "CLIMBING BRANCHES"

This should be a fun class that explains how to plan a family reunion to renew lost contacts, introduce new ones and celebrate your heritage. Discuss invitations, get-to-know-you games, gifts, banners, matching clothing items, locations, food, entertainment, cost, kids activities, housing, and ideas for video presentations and scrapbooks.

"MARRIAGE AND FAMILY RELATIONS" OR "PARENTING PRIMER"

Check out the Church's book entitled "Marriage and Family Relations Teacher Guide" for great ideas. You could even invite the teacher of that course in your ward to teach a lesson and share highlights from that course.

"FAMILY SECRETS"

Teach sisters how to create their own family recipe books, showing different techniques for binding and collecting favorite recipes from their extended family members. Not only are family recipe books a great resource for meal planning, but they're a great sentimental keepsake.

"ROUND ROBIN"

Sisters will learn how to create a family "Round Robin" letter to improve communication with extended family members. Talk about other family traditions that can enhance of feeling of closeness when family members live far from each other. Did you know there is a National Council on Family Relations? There is also a Senate Committee on Youth, Women and Family Relations.

"ADIOS ANALOG" OR "BURN, BABY, BURN!"

This could be a great hands-on class where sisters bring in their old family video tapes and learn how to convert them into digital DVD's. Even ladies who are technophobic could learn what equipment they would need at home to update their family records. Show how to spice up boring family footage by adding a soundtrack of music or cool transitions. Compare software programs that are designed to help edit and create better home movies.

"DEJA VIEW" OR "PHOTO FIXES"

Teach sisters how to restore old photos and care for heirloom items. Discuss ways to scan photos into a computer and repair them using various software or use paints and special tools to touch up damaged photos and correct flaws. It would be fun to set up a staging area where sisters could bring their families and have an old fashioned family photo taken with period costumes in black and white or sepia design.

"LOOKING THROUGH THE CRACKS"

Introduce sisters to the Church's genealogy name extraction program. Every ward and stake should have a family history consultant who could teach the sisters how to do name extraction work. Your ward might even have someone who has been called to do this specific work.

"BINDING BINDERS"

Help sisters create a Family Proclamation binder for their own family to use for Family Home Evening or family scripture study time. Divide the Proclamation into topical sections and provide additional written insights that could be used to enhance study of that particular topic. Offer creative tips for parents to teach these important principles to their children.

"CALENDAR COMMUNICATIONS"

Design creative family calendars that the sisters can take home and start using to keep their families' activities more organized. Talk about color-coding children's calendar items as well as clothing, backpacks, special toys, and other items, to help organize young children who can't read yet. Discuss how calendaring can be done during Family Council and how to use techno gadgets to keep track of everyone's schedules. Display different kinds of calendars and show sisters how to make a calendar using family photos for each month that could be given as Christmas gifts to start off a new year.

"ARE WE THERE YET?"

Share ideas for great family vacations. Find a travel agent to talk about different kinds of family trips such as resorts, all-inclusive, family camps, adventure trips, Dude Ranches, and other locations that specialize in family service and activities. Invite someone who has gone to the Church's Aspen Grove camp in Utah to share photos and experiences. Discuss special needs of traveling with children, how to pack, and inexpensive options for family vacation time.

"DATE NIGHT" OR "RELATIONSHIP RESCUE" OR "TABLE FOR TWO"

Find a creative teacher to share inexpensive and memorable ideas for date nights the sisters can plan with their hubbies. Talk about the importance of regular date nights, how to reignite the flame in a marriage, babysitting, communication games to play while eating at a restaurant, and creative invitations to enhance the anticipation of date night. Invite a few husbands to play "The Newlywed Game" with their wives.

"ADDICTED TO SCRAPBOOKING"

Need I say more? This could be a fun workshop-type class where sisters could bring photographs and learn how to put a page or two together using creative, new techniques. Surely you have a sister in your ward who is known as the Scrapbooking Queen and could teach this class! The teacher could show some of the latest ideas and tools as well as teach beginners how to start. Invite a local scrapbooking store to give away samples and supply some of the tools for the evening.

"MEMORABLE MOMENTS"

Talk about great family traditions that unify and create a sense of belonging and security. This can be a really fun class with lots of examples, ideas, and sharing. Discuss daily rituals, holiday celebrations and how to blend traditions in mixed families.

"PICTURE PERFECT"

Learn how to properly hang and display pictures of family and ancestors in your home. Talk about how to attractively display photo collections on a wall, how to create an appealing grouping of photos on tables, and how to frame and mat pictures.

"MOTHER OF THE YEAR"

Contact your local chapter of the American Mothers, Inc. and invite the "Mother of the Year" or "Young Mother of the Year" from your state to speak to your sisters about the nobility in motherhood. Find out what mothers are doing in your community to make the world a better place. Be sure to check out the ideas found on www.americanmothers.org.

"AFTER THE MARRIAGE ENDS"

Find a caring teacher to discuss divorce in a very sensitive way and talk about being single again in the Church. This class should help sisters deal with feelings of loss, denial, guilt, rejection, anger and move toward acceptance, understanding and the ability to love again. Depending on the needs of the sisters in your Relief Society, this class could be geared towards helping those going through a divorce or how to understand and support loved ones who are.

"EYE ON GOVERNMENT" OR "FOR THE PEOPLE"

Become literate about legislation affecting gospel values such as marriage and the family, religious symbols on federal property, prayer, etc. Help the sisters know what they can do to make a difference and have their voices be heard. Teach them where they need to register to become voters.

FAMILY HOME EVENING

"FAMILY HOME EVENING 101"

Set up a room in the church to look like a living room and have a pretend Family Home Evening. Teach newly baptized members what's included in holding one. Offer sisters the manual and videos so they can get started in their homes. Teach them about all of the resources where they can go to get ideas for lessons such as the Church magazines, Sunday school manuals, the Internet, Gospel Essentials book, Gospel Art Picture Kit, church videos, and, of course, the scriptures!

Prepare family home evening packets with visual aids, copies of songs, recipe ideas for refreshments, suggested scripture reading, and inspiring stories for all ages. Have experienced sisters share some of their most memorable and successful family home evening ideas.

"FABULOUS FAMILY HOME EVENING IDEAS"

This class should be a great brainstorm of ideas to help sisters prepare lessons and fun activities for their families. You could divide sisters into age groups for young children, older children, and singles. Have sisters share their great successes as well as blunders to remind them that families' needs are ever changing and growing and that there is no one way to have a good family home evening! Discuss great places to go in your area for fun family excursions and present a lot of ideas for family service projects.

"FAMILY HOME EVENING CHARTS"

Sisters love cute charts that help organize assignments for family home evening, so this class could show them all different kinds of charts from refrigerator magnet displays to wooden houses with pegs to hang family names to simple paper calendars or elaborate computer spreadsheets. Have sisters make one to take home for their families.

"CAMCORDER CREATIONS"

Show sisters how they can make their own video productions of scripture stories or famous church history moments with their families for a fun and memorable Family Home Evening or Sunday activity. Talk about different kinds of equipment and how to avoid common filming mistakes. Have the sisters use props and wear costumes that night to make a movie together that they could then share with their families.

"SACRED SITES"

Invite sisters who have been to famous church sites to share reports on each location so that the ladies could return to their families and create a great Family Home Evening about Church history.

"PUPPET PALS"

Make cute puppets that could be used during Family Home Evening lessons. Show different kinds of puppets as well as models for puppet theaters that could be made at home. You could also make one puppet to represent each member of the family to use during role-plays and Family Councils.

"TEMPLE PAGEANT"

Find someone who has performed in one of the many temple pageants to share experiences and explain how to get involved in one for next summer. It would be great to show a video of one of the performances and talk about what a great testimony-building experience it is for the youth.

"FAMILY COUNCILS"

This is a "how to" class that teaches sisters how to hold a Family Council with their own families. Talk about different ways to conduct this meeting, as well as certain items that should be included in order to make it a positive experience for all ages.

"MOM, I'M BOARD"

Create home-made board games that the sisters can take home and play with their families during Family Home Evening. Show different kinds of games that could be adjusted to fit a family lesson on any gospel topic. Share ideas for making up their own trivia questions and rules.

"IF YE ARE PREPARED YE SHALL NOT FEAR"

Well, you may not get an entire year's worth of Family Home Evening lessons in one night, but you could get a good jump start on them by organizing a group of interested sisters to form a Family Home Evening packet club. Each sister prepares several copies of one lesson, including visual aids, recipe ideas, stories, a game, a scripture plaque to hang on the refrigerator for the week and anything else the ladies want included in the packets. This class could teach sisters how to prepare the packets or could be a time when they bring their material and share it with one another.

"THREE-FOLD MISSION OF THE CHURCH"

Offer a lesson on the "Three-Fold Mission of the Church" which includes: *Perfect the Saints, Proclaim the Gospel,* and *Redeem the Dead.* Provide ideas for the sisters to present the material to their families in a creative Family Home Evening lesson.

FAMILY PRAYER

"THE EFFECTUAL FERVENT PRAYER"

Have a lesson on how to better teach our children to pray. Prepare a Family Home Evening packet with visual aids, object lessons, and stories that emphasize the importance of prayer and how to pray. Talk about how our prayers are different when we serve as a mouthpiece for family prayer or in other group settings. Discuss the proper language of prayers (thee, thine, thy, thou.)

"PRAYER CHARTS"

Create a decorative family chart to keep track of whose turn it is to be the voice at family prayer time. Show charts that young children can use when they are learning to pray every day.

"FASTING AND PRAYER"

Teach the importance of fasting when combined with prayer and share stories from the scriptures that illustrate when and why it should be done. Help sisters learn how to help their families have more meaningful Fast Sundays.

FAMILY SCRIPTURE STUDY

"SCRIPTURE STUDIES"

Have sisters prepare a Family Home Evening lesson complete with visual aids, object lessons, scriptures, stories, etc that could be used to teach their families the importance of scripture study. Share examples of how families can study the scriptures together in different ways. Let sisters know which scriptures are being studied this year in Sunday School, Seminary, or the local Institute so they can coordinate their studies with one of those courses if they would like to. Invite a Seminary or Primary teacher to share ideas on teaching the scriptures to children.

"SETTING THE MARK"

Make creative bookmarks for each member of the family to use in his/her scriptures. Show different styles of bookmarks and use a crafting technique that the sisters are interested in learning, such as dried flowers, gold-leafing, stamping, or faux painting. Share ideas for scripture reading plans and different ways you can mark favorite scripture passages.

"HOLD FAST TO THE WORD"

Make paper dolls, puppets, or figures on pop-sickle sticks that could be used during Family Home Evening as visual aids when learning about certain people in the scriptures.

"SCRIPTURE MASTERY"

Encourage families of Seminary students to memorize the Scripture Mastery verses that are being taught this year. Design creative charts and posters to help memorize them. Invite Seminary students to show the sisters fun memorizing tricks. Offer prizes to the sisters who can memorize them! Have a Seminary instructor teach the ladies how to hold a Scripture Chase contest with their families.

"CHARTS GALORE"

Make creative charts for keeping track of scripture study individually or as a family. Share charts and timelines that could be made to coordinate with a certain course of study. Show sisters how to create posters, graphs, checklists, diagrams and other illustrations to help their families' scripture study.

"COSTUME CREATIONS" OR "BRINGING THE SCRIPTURES TO LIFE"

If you're like me, you love costumes and know that they can

add a fun spark to any lesson. Help the sisters make different kinds of costumes and props they can use with their families, such as an armor of God, Bible-time tunics and robes, leather pouches and belts, Lamanite swords and scabbards, and other adornments that show the latest fashions from earlier centuries. Invite some children to play dress-up and provide a Scripture Duds fashion show.

"FEAST ON THE WORD"

Have a lesson and "Taster's Table" of foods from the Bible. Create special dishes using dates, figs, olives, etc. You could also have a "Smell Session" where sisters could smell common Bible fragrances such as frankincense, myrrh, cardamom, etc. Share recipes so the sisters can make scripture meals at home for their families. Have sisters bake this "Scripture Cake." Ingredients:

3/4 cup Genesis 18:8
1 1/2 cup Jeremiah 6:20
5 Isaiah 10:14 (separated)
3 cups sifted Leviticus 24:5
3 teaspoons 2 Kings 2:20
3 teaspoons Amos 4:5
1 teaspoon Exodus 3:23
1/4 teaspoon each 2 Chronicles 9:9
1/2 cup Judges 4:19
3/4 cup chopped Genesis 43:11
3/4 cup finely cut Jeremiah 24:5
3/4 cup 2 Samuel 16:1
Whole Genesis 43:11

Cream Genesis 18 with Jeremiah 6. Beat in yolks of Isaiah 10, one at a time. Sift together Leviticus 24; 2 Kings 2; Amos 4; Exodus 30; and 2 Chronicles 9. Blend into creamed mixture alternately with Judges 4. Beat whites of Isaiah 10 till stiff; fold in. Fold in chopped Genesis 43; Jeremiah 24; and 2 Samuel 16. Turn into 10-inch tube pan that has been greased and dusted with Leviticus 24. Bake at 325 degrees F until it is golden brown or Gabriel blows his trumpet, whichever happens first. Bake for an hour and ten minutes. Remove from oven. Cool, serve and enjoy!

"GOSPEL GAMES"

Design games that could be played on Sundays or during Family Home Evening that test scripture skills. You could use multiple choice and true/false tests from the Friend magazine as well as crossword puzzles, Scripture Hangman, and timed sessions. Try making cards to play scripture charades, Tic-Tac-Know, or a Seminary-style Scripture Chase. Teach sisters how to create dot-to-dot drawings for their young children.

"TREE OF LIFE"

Have each sister create a "Tree of Life" that she could take home and use with her family. The trees could be designed to be flat on a wall hanging, poster or chart or they could be crafted to be three dimensional, using paper tubes, cardboard, paper, and other materials. When someone in the family does something good to spread the love of Christ add a fruit (or something to resemble the items in Lehi's Dream) to the boughs on the tree. Talk about the symbolism found in 1 Nephi chapters 8 to 15 and how this project in our home could remind us of the love of God and the gift of His son, Jesus Christ.

PARENTING SKILLS

"PARENTING 101"

Invite a speaker to share parenting tips for children of all ages or offer several classes for different ages of children to address specific needs of development. Provide lots of practical solutions as well as tips for improving communication, building positive relationships, and discipline. Talk about how to raise a confident, loving, and giving child.

"PARENTING PROBLEMS"

Hold a book review on various parenting books. Talk about parenting advice that is offered in the scriptures. Listen to some clips from some of the many great books on tape and CD. Discuss common problem areas in parenting such as chores, allowance, homework, and bedtime.

"DR. MOM"

Invite a pediatrician to share developmental insights to children's health and teach moms some tips as they graduate from diaper rash to skinned knees to training bras. Talk about how to choose a good pediatrician and family doctor. Discuss the guidelines for immunizations that are required in your state.

"MOVIE MADNESS"

This class could be a review about good family-friendly flicks. Provide a list of great family classics and how to help children avoid peer pressure to watch movies that are inappropriate. Talk about some of the technology parents can use to clean up the TVs in their own home (filters, TV Guardian, locks, "Clean Flicks," etc.) Form a "clean" video club for sisters who are interested in swapping good movies with one another.

"BIRTH ORDER: SCIENCE OR MYTH?" OR "SENSE OR NONSENSE"

Offer a class that discusses birth order personalities in children and yourself. Learn about the psychology behind different character traits. Check out these web sites for interesting personality studies: www.discoveryourpersonality.com, www.paladinexec.com or www.teamtechnology.co.uk/tt/h-articl/mb-simpl.htm

"AND EVERYTHING NICE"

Host a Mother/Daughter evening. There are so many sweet themes that can be used to create a memorable evening and one that both young and old will enjoy. Remember to be mindful of the sisters who do not have daughters. Classes that are sure to please all ages could include: hair styling, make-up, a fashion show, baking desserts, scrapbooking, and jewelry making. A fun memento from the evening would be to decorate an area to be used as a backdrop for a mother/daughter photograph using a Polaroid camera that would produce an instant picture or a digital camera that could be printed out during the evening. It would also be sweet to have the daughters make short presentations about why they love their mothers or what lessons they have learned from them.

"MAMA'S BOY"

Fair is fair. If you're going to host a Mother/Daughter evening you should think about doing a Mother/Son one as well! You could focus on missionary training skills, cooking and sewing basics, play volleyball or other fun games, do a bake-off or other fun "guy games," how to make tasty treats with disgusting names (so the boys will like them) such as those worm in dirt pudding cups. (I have four boys who love those!)

"STRANGER DANGER"

Help sisters know how to teach their children about strangers, self-defense, crime prevention, Internet dangers, and how to avoid potentially dangerous situations. Ask your local police department to give some of those fingerprint kits for mothers to take home and do with their children. Blockbuster also has a video ID program they could tell mothers about. Learn more about Meagan's Law in your state.

"TREASURES OF THE HEART"

Invite sisters to bring an heirloom to share about a female ancestor that has inspired them. Talk about how to care for and display such items. Share stories and talk about traditions to start in your families that instill a sense of belonging.

"SAFE SPACE"

The instructor for this class would teach how to child-proof your home, showing samples of products available and discussing how to avoid common accidents that occur inside and outside.

"PARENTS, THE ANTI-DRUG"

Invite a local narcotics agent to teach the sisters how to protect themselves and their families against drugs. It would be interesting to have a demonstration of those drug dogs that work with the policemen and talk about what signs to look for in behavior to tell if a loved one is getting involved in drugs.

"DIAMOND IN THE ROUGH"

This class helps parents learn how to discover their children's hidden talents and help them blossom. Talk about after-school programs that are available in your area, clubs, community classes, music lessons, leadership development courses, 4-H, Junior Achievement, and other organizations that help build character and skills in your children.

"BABYSITTING BOX"

Moms could make a special box for their babysitters that would include emergency information, first aid guidelines, important phone numbers, special comforting toys, a cassette tape of the mom reading a favorite story to calm a sad child, etc. Have someone talk about how to select a good babysitter, the going rate of pay, safety concerns, guidelines for fathers, and expectations.

"TEACHING MOMENTS" OR "BACK TO SCHOOL"

Invite a school teacher to help parents understand how they can help their children get the most out of their education and how to better communicate with the teachers. Talk about expectations, PTA involvement, homework help, and parent/teacher interviews. Share ideas about how to use teaching moments at home to reinforce what is being taught at school.

"BUILDING FAITH"

Have the president of each of the auxiliaries at church (Primary, Cub Scouts, Achievement Days, Young Men, Boy Scouts, Young Women, Sunday School) share what is going on in that particular program and how mothers can help their children build faith and testimonies. Learn about the goal programs in the other auxiliary organizations of the church and how parents can help children achieve their goals and awards.

"MISSION POSSIBLE"

This class could be to help mothers know how to prepare their sons and daughters to serve full-time missions and create a "Missionary Training Center" atmosphere in their homes. Invite an instructor from the MTC to describe a typical day in the MTC for the missionaries and how to prepare their children to enter the mission field. Talk about how mothers can overcome sadness of a child being away from home by being constructive and showing support through letters, care packages, e-mails and phone calls. Talk about mission rules and what should be expected of a missionary mom. This class could also include a focus on preparing older couples to serve missions.

"E-MOM"

Invite an experienced computer nerd to share tips on Internet safety, how to monitor the history on your child's computer, and how to protect your children from spam. Compare different child safety programs and talk about the common tricks those rotten cyber predators use to lure children on-line. Check out "Citizens For Community Values" which aggressively fights on-line porn, as well as www.spamcop.net, mail washer programs, your local Sheriff's office, and find out if your state honors "Meagan's Law" to allow citizens to look on public maps and records to see if sex offenders live in their neighborhood.

"HAPPY BIRTHDAY TO YOU!"

Every mom needs this class! Talk about how to throw a great birthday party for children and teens. Discuss how many guests to invite according to the age of the child, when (and when not to) invite guests of the opposite sex, successful party games, party favors, entertainment, invitations, thank you cards and food. Show how to make balloon animals.

"THE BABYSITTERS' CLUB"

Rather than paying hard-earned money, form a babysitting club using tickets that are exchanged for each hour someone babysits a child. Children's ages determine how many tickets will paid. The group decides how many tickets will be given out when the Babysitting Club is started. After that, moms earn more tickets by watching others' children. Tickets are paid to the mom who baby-sits.

"FUN IN THE SUN"

Invite mothers to share which summer activities were big hits with their children and which ones were a waste of time and money. Talk about different kinds of summer camps, as well as how to register your teens in "Especially For Youth," BYU Education Week, and organize those cool pioneer treks.

"LDS SOCIAL SERVICES"

Invite the people from the Church's Social Services Department to share what resources are available to unwed mothers, single parents, couples wanting to adopt, help for wayward children, and marriage counseling.

"OH BABY!"

This could be a fun class if you have a lot of newlyweds and soon-to-be-moms in your ward. Talk about prenatal care, infant massage, what items out of the suggested "layette" are really needed, post-partum depression, breast feeding, etc.

CHAPTER SEVEN
Strengthening Relationships

Matthew 5:38-44 "Ye have heard that it hath been said, An eye for an eye, and a tooth for a tooth;

But I say unto you, That ye resist not evil: but whosoever shall smite thee on they right cheek, turn to him the other also.

And if any man will sue thee at the law, and take away thy coat, let him have thy cloke also.

And whosoever shall compel thee to go a mile, go with him twain.

Give to him that asketh thee, and from him that would borrow of thee turn not thou away.

Ye have heard that it hath been said, Thou shalt love thy neighbor, and hate thine enemy.

But I say unto you, Love your enemies, bless them that curse you, do good to them that hate you, and pray for them which despitefully use you, and persecute you."

Matthew 25:40 "And the King shall answer and say unto them, Verily I say unto you, Inasmuch as ye have done it unto one of the least of these my brethren, ye have done it unto me."

COMMUNICATION AND RESOLVING CONFLICTS

"ROMANCING THE STONE"

Learn how to show love to people who are often hard to love. Talk about how to understand and communicate with difficult people, whether they be family members, colleagues at work, teachers at school or wherever.

"SWEET NOTHINGS"

Show the sisters how to make candy grams for their families using candy bars on a poster to replace certain words in a loving letter. Share other ideas for using store bought candies to leave loving mementos for family members. Replace those white slips of paper in Hershey's kisses with love notes you make on your own. Learn how to make cookie bouquets and other edible expressions of appreciation and love.

"MNM TIME"

In my house "MnM Time" stands for "Me and Mom," a special time when I visit with each of my children individually and go over their goals, finances, and more. I know "Me and Mom" isn't grammatically correct, but it gives us an excuse to eat MnM's and sit and talk for as long as we want! Have a teacher share other ways to get children talking, how to make "Lap Chat" folders to record progress on goals, how to interview your children, and ideas that improve communication.

"RELATION SHIP"

Use a nautical theme to decorate and talk about how a family works together like a crew, including the Captain (Dad), First Mate (Mom), Purser, Seamen, (children) . . . you get the idea. Talk about how to delegate responsibilities and how to motivate children to work. Some families create Chairmen of different "committees" that have to be reported on during Family Council such as "Social," "Family Home Evening Director," "Service Specialist," Time Management Tsar, etc.

"OVER THE RIVER AND THROUGH THE WOODS"

This is a fun class full of ideas on how to keep grandparents in touch with the growing children. It can be geared toward the mothers or the grandmothers. Talk about ways to use e-mail, digital photos, tape cassettes, camcorders, and other tools to keep information flowing and invitations extended to attend recitals, games and other important functions.

"MEN ARE FROM MARS"

This class takes a fun look at the differences between men and women and how to both celebrate and understand them! Learn about how to communicate better and understand each other's "love language."

"THE PEN IS MIGHTIER THAN THE SWORD"

Learn how to do calligraphy to beautify your letters, certificates, awards, place-cards, wall décor, and more to enhance your written communication.

"BEST FRIENDS FOREVER"

Create friendship bracelets that could be given as special gifts and talk about the importance of having girlfriends. Learn how to balance girlfriend gatherings and "Guy Time" in a marriage, and discuss the proper place for confidences.

"LOVE AT HOME"

Using talks from General Conference, have the teacher talk about ways to create a loving atmosphere in the home.

"ANNUAL FAMILY LETTER"

Offer a class on how to create a good Christmas family letter, warning of common mistakes and pitfalls. There is a careful skill in creating an appealing family letter that is humorous and informative but not boastful and obnoxious. Show samples of good letters and offer creative tips on including photos and graphics.

"PILLOW TALK BOOKS"

A Pillow Talk book is a great way to get children to open up to their parents in a less threatening way. Decorate a small notebook or flat binder that can be kept under a child's pillow. The mom writes loving things in it, including one question that the child has to then answer to keep the "conversation" going.

When the child is finished writing he leaves it under his pillow and later the mom finds it and writes some more as a type of ongoing discussion. A class could include other ideas on how to improve parent/child communication.

"HAND SPEAK"

Find someone who knows sign language to teach the sisters some of the basics. Invite someone from your local deaf branch to share experiences and help sisters both understand the needs of the deaf community and feel more comfortable trying to communicate with them. Let interested sisters know they can purchase simple sign language books and videos that teach how to use gospel terminology from the Church Distribution Center.

"A TISKET, A TASKET"

Teach sisters how to make attractive, yet inexpensive gift baskets based on themes. You could also teach them how to put small gifts inside those giant balloons and other creative gift-wrapping techniques. Have sisters make special Mother's Day baskets for single moms or for military moms whose husbands are overseas.

"NEUTRAL CORNERS"

There are disagreements in even the most perfect of marriages. The trick is learning how to "fight fair." Teach sisters how to resolve conflicts in marriage without hurting the relationship. Talk about timing, communication tips, and words that should never be used.

"MUSHY STUFF"

This is a fun class that encourages the sisters to be creative in expressing their feelings to their loved ones by writing love notes, through e-mail, poetry, and romantic games. Talk about traditions that create loving bonds such as writing a special birthday letter to your children each year. Teach sisters how to make home-made cards using rubber stamp techniques or other crafting methods the sisters are interested in learning how to do.

"RELIEF SOCIETY GREETINGS UNPLUGGED"

Have the sisters record a video of their greetings and salutations to those sisters who cannot regularly attend Enrichment Night due to illness or other circumstances. Copies of the video could be sent to homebound sisters or even to those who have recently moved away from the ward to keep the lines of communication open and to share sisterhood.

"FAMILY FEUD"

Have sisters create teams of "families" and play a version of Family Feud with answers to questions that ward members have reported on such as "Who is your favorite latter-day prophet? What is your favorite temple? What was the best ward activity we've ever had?" etc. Include a lesson on how families can resolve conflicts and use Family Council time to work through problems.

"IM IQ"

Teach sisters to understand the new lingo their kids are using for Instant Messenger or on their pagers and cell phones. Talk about safety issues for pagers, phones, and the Internet.

"PEN PALS"

Find another ward in another state or country that would like to be Pen Pals with the sisters in your ward. Learn about their language and culture. Sisters could send letters individually or the Relief Society could send one general letter with pictures of the ladies.

REPENTANCE AND FORGIVENESS

"THE MIRACLE OF FORGIVENESS"

Discuss the book "The Miracle of Forgiveness" by Spencer W. Kimball. Have the sisters write about a personal experience with repentance in a journal page and share experiences when they have felt the sweet peace of forgiveness. Share tips on teaching children about forgiveness and repentance.

"POWER TO FORGIVE"

Discuss the dangers of holding grudges, gossip, reconciliation, resolving anger and restoring hope. Talk about guilt and how to achieve personal peace when you need to forgive yourself from past mistakes.

"GUILT RIDDEN"

Learn how to forgive yourself and overcome guilt. Latter-day Saint women tend to be really good at feeling guilt over things they haven't done enough of (genealogy, bake home-made bread every day, run a marathon before taking children to Seminary, etc) and often don't give themselves credit for all of the good things they do. Discuss how to rid yourself of feelings of inadequacy and become empowered by acknowledging your efforts.

"LOAN FORGIVENESS" OR
"STARVING COLLEGE STUDENTS"

Learn about educational loans for students, loan repayment, and student aid. Talk about scholarships that are available and other ways to avoid getting in debt.

EFFECTIVE LEADERSHIP

"SHEEP HERDER VS. SHEPHERD"

Using Christ's example, discuss effective leadership skills and "Shadow Leadership."

"MOSES-STYLE LEADERSHIP"

Talk about how to delegate and show examples of how it was effectively used by prophets, such as Moses. Help mothers learn how they can delegate chores and assignments in their homes to teach their children certain skills.

"SWEET SIXTIES"

Spotlight the older sisters in your ward and share a little bit about their lives so the younger sisters can get to know them. Your "Golden Oldies" sisters can be a tremendous resource for leadership ideas and experiences. They can also give you great ideas for successful Enrichment Nights they have seen over the years!

"OH WHAT A RELIEF"

Invite the Relief Society presidency and leaders of the other auxiliaries to talk about the lessons they have learned while serving as leaders. Talk about how to work in a presidency and merge different leadership styles.

"GUESS WHO'S COMING TO DINNER?"

Have someone teach a class on how to host a dinner party. Share tips on how to create an elegant dinner without spending a lot of money. You could also give creative ideas on how to throw a more casual backyard BBQ, a pool party, neighborhood potluck, or other events where you open your home to company and want them to feel welcome and comfortable. Discuss how to lead a dinner conversation so that guests are interested and appreciated.

"OOOH BABY BABY!"

Teach a class on how to throw a baby shower. The teacher could share photographs, food samples, money-saving tips, and ideas on how to decorate and entertain. A short lesson on party etiquette could be included, as well as do's and don'ts for party games. You could even throw a mini-party for a sister in your ward who is expecting a baby. The sisters could also share some of their favorite gift ideas, including how to lead guests to coordinate a group gift.

"I DO!"

This class would be a fun lesson on how to throw a bridal shower or wedding reception for someone. Wedding do's and don'ts could be discussed, as well as popular trends, creative table decorations, menu selection, gift registry, music and all things nuptial. Don't forget something borrowed and something blue! Discuss how to show leadership without upstaging the bride.

"THE PERFECT MATCH"

Invite the Relief Society sisters from the Single Ward to share an Enrichment night with your ward. Focus on the sisterhood that can be shared. Encourage the single sisters to show leadership in conducting some of the classes and emphasize that everyone can learn something from one another. Plan get-to- know-you games with the sisters.

"PARTY ANIMAL"

This could be a fun evening where all of the classes teach sisters different aspects of throwing parties such as making cute invitations and thank you cards, decorating on a budget, food, party favors, games, entertainment, etc. This is a great evening for ideas if done right before all of the holidays. You could also talk about how to show gracious leadership and host parties for other seasonal events like Valentine's Day, Cinco de Mayo, Fourth of July, etc.

"BACK TO SCHOOL"

Invite a former or current PTA President to talk about her experiences while serving in a leadership position in the school. Talk about how to get involved as a volunteer for the school or in the classroom, as well as show leadership in other organizations such as Cub Scouts, Girl Scouts, campus clubs, Team Mom for sports, etc.

"RAISING LEADERS FOR TOMORROW"

Offer a lesson for mothers to learn how they can prepare their children to be effective leaders at school, in sports, in the mission field, and with their friends. Talk about peer pressure, organizations that encourage youth leadership, and how to help a shy child show strength.

"CELEBRATING SUCCESS"

Study biographies of successful leaders, visionaries and celebrities to find out what the keys are to success and good leadership. Discuss tips for good management, women in leadership roles, personal discipline, and skills that are necessary to motivate and inspire others.

CHAPTER EIGHT

Self-Reliance

D&C 88:119 "Organize yourselves; prepare every needful thing; and establish a house, even a house of prayer, a house of fasting, a house of faith, a house of learning, a house of glory, a house of order, a house of God."

HOME STORAGE AND EMERGENCY PREPAREDNESS

"NOAH'S ARK"

Have sisters learn about all of the different methods for storing food supplies in their homes. Share ideas for creative storage such as underneath beds, behind curtains, under skirted tables, etc. This could also be a hands-on workshop where sisters could build food storage rolling shelves to take home.

"SELF RELIANCE"

Talk about the importance of self-reliance in God's plan and how it fits into the Church's Welfare program. Share quotes from

Ralph Waldo Emerson's writings on self-reliance and discuss the balance of trusting in God versus relying on man. Help sisters feel empowered by offering them tools to be more self-reliant.

(SEE IDEAS UNDER "PRESERVING FOOD" ON PAGE 60)

"ANOTHER MAN'S TREASURE"

Learn the ins and outs of having a garage sale to get rid of all that junk once and for all! Talk about how to prepare, price and display items. Any sisters who want to get rid of their junk NOW could bring it to Enrichment Night and you could have a mini-garage sale.

"ABC'S OF CPR" OR "HEART SMART"

Offer a course where the sisters could become CPR certified so they will know what to do in an emergency. Classes are often offered by your local fire department, at a hospital, or through the health department and usually last several hours long. You could offer a mini-class without the certification or the Enrichment Night class could be part one of a series of nights when sisters receive instruction toward their certification.

"DR. MOM"

Invite a local paramedic, nurse or doctor to teach sisters basic guidelines for first aid. Sisters could also make first aid kits for their 72-hour emergency bags or for their cars. You could also invite a scout leader to share what information is taught to scouts to earn their "First Aid" merit badge. Learn how to treat choking, stings, burns, cuts, and other common injuries. Discuss the Good Samaritan Law and how to treat yourself if no one is around to help.

"MOTHER NATURE" OR "BACK TO BASICS"

Learn about how to recycle, how to store items, and how to use composts.

"ARMED ARMY OF GOD"

Collect items to provide a 72-hour kit for the full-time missionaries serving in your ward or branch. It could be a large kit that stays in their apartment or a small one that they take with them when they get transferred to another area.

"SURVIVOR"

Using the theme of the popular reality TV show "Survivor" review basic survival skills. There is a great "Worse Case Scenario" book series which has also been turned into a board game that you can use to see how well prepared the sisters are. You could also show a few video clips from the "How To Survive" series on TV. Hand out prizes for sisters who actually have a 72-hour kit in their car that night.

"WHAT'S THE NUMBER FOR 9-1-1?"

Have sisters create charts and lists with emergency phone numbers to keep by their phones. Include phone numbers for Bishop's, Home Teachers, Visiting Teachers and presidents of each auxiliary. Provide a laminator for the sisters to use to make their lists waterproof. Remind sisters about the phone chain you have for your ward. Share ideas for families to create a secret code only they know for emergency situations. Find out if your ward leadership has a list of which members have chainsaws, trucks, small boats, generators, and other equipment that might be needed in an emergency. If such a list doesn't exist, create one!

"SAFE SPACE"

The instructor for this class would teach how to child-proof your home, showing samples of products available and discussing how to avoid common accidents that occur inside and outside.

"WHEN SPARKS FLY"

Invite the Fire Department to teach a lesson on fire safety. They often have a "Smoke House" they can bring where the sisters can actually go inside and see what it's like to be in a smoky house and try to get out (the demonstration is safe, but be mindful of sisters with asthma). Have the sisters actually practice climbing a safety ladder or how to use a fire extinguisher. Talk about carbon monoxide and radon detectors. Decorate with Dalmations, engines, ladders, etc. Help sisters plan various escape routes from their home during fire or other emergencies. Your local firemen will most likely be happy to bring those cute plastic firemen helmets and some coloring books for the moms to take home to their children.

"WHEN DISASTER STRIKES"

Invite someone from your local FEMA office to talk to the sisters about the natural disasters that are most likely to occur in your area, whether they be tornadoes, hurricanes, earthquakes, floods, or brush fires. Find out what precautions are in place and how families can be better prepared. Learn about what kinds of city alarms exist for your town and how you can help others around you. After living through the San Diego fires last year in southern California, several stakes created a very practical guide for members entitled "What We Learned From The Fires." See if such a guide exists for common disasters in your area.

"TOOLS THAT SAVE"

Teach sisters about smoke alarms, radon detectors, carbon monoxide alarms, fire extinguishers and other life-saving items to keep in your home. Discuss routine maintenance and how to tell the difference between good ones and junky ones.

"HANDS ON SAFETY" OR "A FIGHTING CHANCE"

Learn about self-defense in and out of the home. You could even invite a martial arts teacher to come and teach the sisters a few practical moves. Talk about various kinds of personal safety equipment such as pepper sprays and stun guns, using common sense, and how listening to the Spirit can be your best protection.

"CRIME PREVENTION"

The teacher for this class needs to be sensitive to the sisters by creating awareness without overly frightening them. There are so many things one can do to deter criminals from choosing your house or car, such as adding light or motion sensors to exterior lights, hanging a "Guard Dog" sign on your fence even if you don't have a dog, adding safety locks, using random light timers inside when you're on vacation, etc. Your local policeman would be happy to speak to the sisters and usually has written information they can take home to evaluate the level of security in their own homes.

"FIVE OF THEM WERE WISE"

Review the parable of the Ten Virgins in Matthew 25:1-13 and discuss its relevance today. There is a beautiful painting about this parable and artist's booklet that can add further insight to your lesson. Talk about the importance of being prepared in all things.

EDUCATION AND RESOURCE MANAGEMENT

"BACK TO SCHOOL NIGHT" OR "MAKING THE GRADE"

Welcome the ladies back to school, complete with cafeteria trays and ladies in hair nets serving the refreshments! Fun classes could include: How to make creative and healthy sack lunches for your family, communicating with your child's teacher, PTA involvement, homework helps, and household management.

"EASY E-BAY"

Have someone who is Internet-savvy teach the sisters how to buy and sell on E-Bay as well as other Internet sites. Discuss the hazards and safety concerns.

Discuss other ways ladies can make money on-line by doing market research studies and e-mail reading programs that earn you awards.

"CAMPUS CO-EDS"

Invite returning college students to share some of their experiences while away at school. Discuss what is happening around campuses these days and how the sisters could take advantage of performances and other events. Offer a list of adult classes that are being taught in your community for sisters who would like to advance in their education or just take some fun classes. Talk about the program BYU has for women to finish degrees that were once started there as well as independent programs offered at other universities.

"MAKING CENTS"

Teach the sisters how to prepare a household budget. Discuss ways to earn and save money. Show various kinds of charts to help analyze family spending. Discuss ways sisters can use their talents at home to earn extra spending money such as teaching piano lessons or any other instrument, tutoring, bookkeeping, sewing designer curtains, etc. Have sisters who are already doing that share their experiences and advice.

"RIGHT ON THE MONEY"

Invite a financial planner or CPA to teach the sisters how to get out of debt, improve their credit rating, and plan for their future. Talk about bankruptcy and how the women can get free copies of their credit report. Teach them how to read their report, how items are recorded and how to correct mistakes.

"MONEY TALKS"

Have a lesson for mothers to learn ways they can teach their children how to earn and save money. Talk about different kinds of savings and checking plans, ATM and debit cards, and how to begin to establish good credit. Sisters could create a special box or piggy bank that shows children how to save for education, mission, and college.

"THE SCOOP ON SCHOLARSHIPS"

Invite a high school counselor or university admissions staff to explain the application process for getting into college and how student aid works. Discuss Sallie Mae, Nellie Mae, FAFSA, and other loan programs for college students. Share tips on submitting applications and essays for scholarships.

"FIVE LITTLE PIGGIES"

Offer classes that go along with each part of this famous nursery rhyme:

- This little piggy went to market (class on stock market and finances, have a Relief Society swap meet where sisters "purchase" donated items, how to select the best fruit and veggies, coupon clipping)

- This little piggy stayed home (home decorating, parenting tips, home-schooling, activities to do with your children).

- This little piggy had roast beef (cooking with ground beef, have a butcher explain cuts of beef, how to cook a great steak, steak and potato recipes).

- This little piggy had none (diet and nutrition, exercise or aerobics class, vegetarian cooking)
- This little piggy went wee, wee, wee all the way home (learn about all the fun things to do in your area, potty-training tips, a class on the importance of humor, have a trained instructor teach voice lessons) Use your imagination and have fun!

"COMPUTER GEEK 101"

Teach sisters some of the basics for computer repair and how to identify certain problems. Discuss different kinds of computers, hardware and software.

"DEALS THAT ARE NIFTY BY SISTER THRIFTY" OR "COUPON QUEEN"

Share ideas on how to save money by clipping coupons, using Internet coupons and other smart shopping tricks. Create an e-mail list for sisters who want to alert each other about bargains around town.

"LIVING SMART" OR "LEGAL MUMBO JUMBO"

Most people don't want to talk about wills, living trusts or legal documents that remind them of their mortality, but it needs to be done in order to protect your loved ones from a real mess after you leave this earthly existence. Invite an attorney to teach the sisters about estates, probate, wills, power of attorney and other documents that need to be drafted as part of your estate planning.

"MONEY MARKET MOMS" OR
"WALL STREET WIVES"

Have sisters learn about stocks, CDs, T-Bills, SLCs, GIC investments, and other securities. Help the women understand financial jargon and various types of instruments in which mutual funds invest.

"HONEY DO" OR "DO IT YOURSELF"

Teach the sisters how to do basic home repair such as how to put a washer in a leaky faucet, calk a bathtub or sink, and seal window frames and door jams so the air won't get through. Learn how to use drills and other tools. Discuss ways to fix a squeaky door or hole in your tile.

"LEMON LAW" OR "MOTOR MOM"

Invite someone from an auto auction to teach the women about buying and selling a car. Discuss the Lemon Law and other protections in your state. Introduce the women to Kelly Blue Book and other auto sites on the Internet to help them make more informed decisions. Compare different forms of auto financing and how to sell a car as a private owner.

"POWDER PUFF MECHANICS"

Invite an auto mechanic to teach the women about basic car maintenance. Have the sisters learn how to change a tire, check the oil in a car, recharge a battery and take care of other auto emergencies. Remind the sisters to wear their grubbies in case they get grease on their clothes.

"PICK ME!"

Have your Ward Employment Specialist share tips on how to successfully interview for a job, how to enter the workforce, how to write an effective resume as well as how to present themselves to their chosen industry. Discussion could include how to submit resume's on-line, working with headhunters, using job search services, asking for a raise, and other techniques for pumping up a career.

"FLEA MARKET FINDS"

Find a sister who loves to go shopping at flea markets, tag sales, thrift stores or consignment shops to share tips on how to spot a good deal and distinguish between quality and junk.

"ANTIQUES ROADSHOW"

Sisters could bring their antiques and heirlooms to have them evaluated by an expert who lives in your area. Discuss how to care for old pieces, polish silver, and display or store precious items so their beauty and value are preserved.

"MYSTERY SHOPPING MOMS"

There are dozens of companies all over the country who will pay people to be mystery shoppers that visit stores and then write short reports about their experience in a particular store, restaurant or other venue. Invite someone who has done assignments to share her experiences and teach the sisters about this industry. You could also have a merchandiser talk about her jobs and how to get assignments. Both fields are great for moms who want to earn a little extra money without committing to a full-time profession outside the home. Talk about certifications that are now available through professional organizations. (MSPA, for example.)

"LOCATION, LOCATION, LOCATION"

Find a real estate agent or broker to share tips on buying, selling, and investing in property. Discuss different kinds of residential and commercial property as well as land and special use sites with lakes, farms, etc.

"YOU'RE NOT THE BOSS OF ME"

Invite owners of small businesses to come and speak to the sisters about what it takes to run a company and how to be a successful entrepreneur. Talk about small business loans, management, employees, tax laws for business owners, franchises, etc.

"WOULD YOU TAKE A CHICKEN?"

Teach sisters about barter clubs across the country and how to get one started in your own ward (if they're interested). Discuss how they operate and how trading services and goods can be especially helpful when money is tight. Suggest other ways to get desired services for free or inexpensively, such as teaching an aerobics class to get a free gym membership, babysitting in exchange for free piano lessons, etc.

HEALTH AND HYGIENE

"THE DOCTOR IS IN"

Invite different kinds of doctors to discuss their areas of specialization from pediatricians to gynecologists to optometrists to family doctors. Talk about when to get immunizations and other annual exams for adults. Share tips on how to choose the right doctor or dentist for your family.

"TOXINS TEST"

Teach sisters about the dangers of common household toxins. Familiarize sisters with what house plants help remove them and how to keep your family and pets safe. Talk about house molds, workplace toxins and how to detoxify your body.

"CHICKEN SOUP FOR THE SOUL" OR "OLD WIVES TALES"

Have a doctor talk about old wives' health remedies and which ones are true and which ones are not. Invite someone from a health food store to share homeopathic remedies.

"GLAMOUR SHOTS"

Make the sisters feel extra special by treating them to a beauty makeover for face and hair and then taking professional photographs of them. Surely you have someone in your ward whose hobby is photography and would set up a mock studio in your building somewhere. Bring lots of flashy jewelry, boas, and fun accessories for the women to play with. What girl doesn't love to dress up?

"TAKE TWO AND CALL ME IN THE MORNING"

Teach sisters how to prepare a year's worth of medical supplies for their families as well as freshly stock their 72-hour kits. Include frequently used medicines, bandages, ointments, cottons, etc. Discuss expiration dates and which medicines are harmful when combined with others.

"MOTHER NATURE" OR "HEALTH FOOD NUTS" OR "SNACK ATTACK"

Have sisters taste samples of healthy alternatives to junk food and high carb snack foods. Discuss nutritional needs and how to get children to reach for the healthy stuff rather than the garbage. Compare popular diets with counsel found in the Word of Wisdom. Introduce the class to different kinds of trail mix, grain bars, dried fruits and veggies, soy, tofu and protein smoothies. Share recipes for making homemade versions.

"DRESS FOR SUCCESS"

You only get one chance to make a first impression. Share expert "Dress for Success" tips for different events. Discuss proper business attire and how to present yourself for a job interview. Learn what to wear to slim your figure, how to recover from a bad hair day, clothing care, proper dress etiquette, wardrobe makeovers, and how to help the men in your life dress for success as well.

"GOOD HEARTED SISTERS"

Invite a cardiologist to share information on how to prevent and reverse heart disease. Discuss blood pressure, diabetes, genetics, how to identify personal risks, advances in technology for treatment, the role of nutrition, and how to help children with congenital heart defects.

"STAND BY YOUR MAN"

Offer a lesson about how to care for the men in your life. Discuss general men's health care, routine exams, how to get your husband to go to the doctor, and caring for your son's healthy development.

"BEATING THE BLUES"

Invite a sensitive teacher to share information about clinical depression and how to recognize it in your loved ones and yourself. Discuss symptoms, treatment, brain chemicals, antidepressants and non-drug therapies, bipolar disorder, post-partum depression, and how to defeat mood disorders with a gospel perspective.

"TESTS YOU DON'T WANT TO CHEAT ON"

Have a doctor or women's health professional discuss regular health exams that should be taken for optimal health and early intervention should illness be found. Discuss tests for cholesterol, blood pressure, blood sugar levels, Pap smears, mammograms, self exams, colonoscopy, cancer screening, and those cool body scan tests that are now available.

"YOU KNOW THE DRILL"

Invite a local dentist to teach the sisters about proper dental care, flossing, preventing serious problems, teeth whitening, orthodontics, gum disease, and how to get your children to brush longer! Most dentists will bring lots of toothbrushes and floss samples if you ask them, as well as some dental care coloring books for the moms to take home to their children.

"SAFE SPACE"

The instructor for this class would teach how to child-proof your home, showing samples of products available and discussing how to avoid common accidents that occur inside and outside.

"A LITTLE OFF THE TOP"

Invite a hair stylist to teach the sisters how to cut their family's hair. Show cute styles for girls and how to dress up their own hair for more elegant occasions. Talk about the organization "Locks of Love" where people who are cutting very long hair can donate it to cancer patients who need wigs.

"ASSISTING AGING PARENTS" OR "GOLDEN OLDIES"

Give sisters practical tools to know how to help aging parents or other loved ones who are experiencing chronic health problems and debilitating illness. Teach the women how to care for care-givers. Discuss nursing homes, hospice, finances, Medicare/Medicaid, and other daily concerns they might need to help with.

"FIGHTING ADDICTION"

With the help of a counselor from Alcoholics Anonymous or another addiction organization, teach the sisters how to help themselves or a loved one who struggles with substance abuse in their lives. This should be a sensitive, informational class with a caring environment and possibly the presence of your Bishop or someone from LDS Social Services.

"WHEN ONLY CHOCOLATE WILL DO"

This lighthearted class helps women learn about and understand PMS. Offer tools to control wacky hormones and mood swings. Sample lots of chocolate. Discuss women's health, menopause, and how to deal with stress without ripping your husband's head off once a month.

"MY FAIR LADY" OR "MISS MANNERS"

This fun class would remind the sisters of proper etiquette and how to teach their children manners for a variety of situations. You could do goofy role-plays demonstrating "do's and don'ts" of proper behavior and crown the sister who answers the most questions correctly as "Miss Manners" for the evening.

"PAMPER NIGHT"

My ward does this every year and the sisters LOVE this! They never want to go home at the end of the evening! We decorate the Cultural Hall with pink tablecloths and flowers so it looks like a real feminine spa. You could also decorate with a relaxing Japanese motif, using lots of natural materials like bamboo, rocks, and water fountains. Each sister gets to pick her first station and can then rotate to the other ones if time allows. Refreshments could include healthy things like fruits & veggies with dip or else you could serve something terribly decadent and make the sisters feel really spoiled. Choices for stations could include: Manicure, Pedicure, Hot wax on hands, feet and elbows, Facial Massage, Make-up tricks and tips, Eyebrow shaping, Skin care, Posture, Hair care.

"RELIEF SOCIETY RUNWAY"

Host a fun fashion show that showcases modest and stylish clothing. Show how to make small adjustments to transform immodest clothing into something you could feel comfortable wearing at Enrichment night (or any place.)

"FOR YOUR EYES ONLY" OR "EYE SEE" OR "THE EYES HAVE IT"

Invite an optometrist to teach sisters about eye care, glasses, lasik surgery, contact lenses, vision screenings for disease, how to choose the right reading glasses, etc. Talk about how keeping an eternal perspective improves our "vision."

CHAPTER NINE

Service

Proverbs 31:20 "She stretcheth out her hand to the poor; yea, she reacheth forth her hands to the needy."

Mosiah 4:26 "And now, for the sake of these things which I have spoken unto you—that is, for the sake of retaining a remission of your sins from day to day, that ye may walk guiltless before God—I would that ye should impart of your substance to the poor, every man according to that which he hath, such as feeding the hungry, clothing the naked, visiting the sick and administering to their relief, both spiritually and temporally, according to their wants."

SERVICE TO FAMILY

"BOX OF LOVE"

Have a class on how to prepare creative, inexpensive care packages to missionaries, college students or military serving far from home. Make copies of jokes and cartoons to include in packages. Tape record greetings from the sisters in the ward. Talk about shipping, postal regulations in other countries, and what items not to ship.

"SECRET PAL"

(PAL = Performing Acts of Love) This is a fun class to give sisters all kinds of creative ideas of things they can do for families and get their children excited about serving one another as well. Have sisters create Secret "PAL" cards that family members can leave for one another when they've performed a secret service. If, for example, a child makes the bed of another family member he would then put this "PAL" card on the bed so that the recipient notices that he was loved! Talk about other "Random Acts of Kindness" that could be performed for family, neighbors and in the community.

"TREE OF LIFE"

Have each sister create a "Tree of Life" that she could take home and use with her family. The trees could be designed to be flat on a wall hanging, poster or chart or they could be crafted to be three dimensional, using paper tubes, cardboard, paper, and other materials. When someone in the family does something good to spread the love of Christ add a fruit (or something to resemble the items in Lehi's Dream) to the boughs on the tree. Talk about the symbolism found in 1 Nephi chapters 8 to 15 and how this project in our home could remind us of the love of God and the gift of His son, Jesus Christ.

"LOVE LETTERS"

Provide a craft table where sisters could create a month's worth of love letters to leave in places around the house that family members could find, such as inside socks, pockets in clothing, drawers, kitchen cabinets, wallets, etc. Use a new crafting technique the sisters would like to learn such as rubber stamping, gold embossing, pressed flowers, or calligraphy.

"SWEET NOTHINGS"

Show the sisters how to make candy grams for their families using candy bars on a poster to replace certain words in a loving letter. Share other ideas for using store bought candies to leave loving mementos for family members. Show the women how to replace those white slips of paper in Hershey's Kisses with special notes you write yourself or how to steam open certain bags of candy that you can slip loving notes inside and then seal back up so nobody can tell it had been previously opened.

"ASSISTING AGING PARENTS" OR "GOLDEN OLDIES"

Give sisters practical tools to know how to help aging parents or other loved ones who are experiencing chronic health problems and debilitating illness. Teach the women how to care for care-givers. Discuss nursing homes, hospice, finances, Medicare/ Medicaid, and other daily concerns they might need to help with.

"A TISKET, A TASKET"

Teach sisters how to make attractive, yet inexpensive gift baskets based on themes. You could also teach them how to put small gifts inside those giant balloons and other creative gift-wrapping techniques. Have sisters make special Mother's Day baskets for single moms or for military moms whose husbands are overseas

SERVICE TO NEIGHBORS

"TAKE A BITE OUT OF CRIME"

Invite the local police department to teach the sisters how they can start a "Neighborhood Watch" in their subdivisions and communities. The police department can bring all kinds of pamphlets and material for the class, as well as provide fun things for the moms to take home to their children that emphasize safety. Discuss crime prevention in and out of the home. Decorate with a dog theme, using ideas from McGruff the Crime Dog and the National Crime Prevention Council.

"NATIONAL NIGHT OUT"

Learn how to organize a "National Night Out" for your neighborhood. Talk to people who have been involved with one before and share information and resources on-line.

"THE ERRAND OF ANGELS"

Share ideas on how to get to know your neighbors and show friendship such as simply caring for a sick mother's child, bringing treats to introduce yourself, inviting them to dinner, hosting a children's party, etc. Have the missionaries share ideas on how to fellowship neighbors and invite them to church functions such as Enrichment Night!

"GUESS WHO'S COMING TO DINNER"

Learn how to host a dinner party. Share tips on how to create an elegant dinner without spending a lot of money. You could also give creative ideas on how to throw a more casual backyard BBQ, a pool party, neighborhood potluck, or other events where you open your home to company and want them to feel welcome and comfortable. Discuss how to lead a dinner conversation so that guests are interested and appreciated.

"BLOCK PARTY"

Talk about how to organize a block party for your neighborhood. You could plan a big celebration for a national holiday such as the 4th of July or Labor Day, or just create an event for an excuse to party! Share ideas on how to fund the fun, plan a parade, get prizes and donations from local vendors, and involve your neighbors by forming a committee.

"BARN RAISING"

Learn how to teach your neighbors about emergency preparedness. Create a phone chain for your block and help neighbors develop a disaster plan. Invite them to go to the Cannery or Bishop's Storehouse with you to can food and learn about food storage. Give sisters courage to know how to talk to their neighbors about being prepared!

"LIKE A GOOD NEIGHBOR"

Teach sisters how to begin fun neighborhood traditions such as the "Halloween Phantom," 12 days of Christmas, "love buckets," and other simple ways they can get neighbors to show kindness to one another throughout the year. Provide a workshop area where sisters can prepare items to anonymously deliver to their neighbors.

SERVICE IN COMMUNITY

"BABY BLANKETS"

Make baby quilts for a local children's hospital or pregnancy crisis center. This could be an on-going project so that over the course of a year several quilts can be made by the sisters and delivered to those in need. Teach the sisters how to start their own quilts at home with their families. Quilts can be given as gifts to college students, missionaries, children's organizations or even sent overseas through the LDS Humanitarian Department.

"A BOY SCOUT IS"

Host a merit badge clinic for boys working towards advancement toward their Eagle Scout award. Sisters could choose an area they could confidently teach by looking at the choices at www. meritbadge.com Teachers need to be officially registered as merit badge counselors in order for the boys to receive credit. Talk to your Scoutmaster to see how you can help.

"FINDING HOPE"

If your area has recently suffered from a natural disaster, find out how you can help those whose homes were destroyed by contacting your local Red Cross, insurance companies, or Salvation Army. Hygiene kits and food stuffs are always needed.

"MILITARY MOMS"

If you live near a military base you probably know how difficult it is for the wives of deployed servicemen to keep things running at home. Have your Relief Society sisters make Easter baskets for the children of soldiers or create special Mother's Day baskets for the women whose husbands won't be there to pamper them on that special day. You can get ideas for other ways you could help by talking to the Chaplain on base or the organization in charge of military wives.

"BLANKET BRIGADE"

Make or gather blankets and coats that could be delivered to the homeless shelters during cold, winter months.

"BOYS & GIRLS CLUB"

Talk to the Director of your local Boys & Girls Club to find out what their current needs are.

"A+" OR "THE GIFT OF LIFE"

Invite your local blood bank or call the American Red Cross to host a blood drive at your church building. Sisters could be volunteers and donors during the evening. Call 1-800-GIVE-LIFE to find out when and where local blood drives are being held.

"THE VOICE OF AMERICA"

Offer to register voters in your area for upcoming elections. Find out how the sisters can help at the booths. Normally there is a training class that volunteers are required to attend. Share ideas about making your voice heard.

"ADOPT A MILE"

Talk to your local city government about their "Adopt A Mile" program and how your sisters could get involved. You will need to commit to cleaning up a certain stretch of a road or waterway for an extended length of time. Be sure to get approval from your Bishop. You could also involve the youth or Primary to help with this ongoing service project.

"NOW GO DO THE RIGHT THING"

Make blankets for the Dr. Laura "My Stuff" bags. She has other projects for abused children and troubled teens that are sponsored by her foundation as well that the sisters might want to get involved with. Check out www.drlaura.com for instructions.

"THANKS IN DEED"

Have sisters write letters to their local Congressmen, media, and school boards to thank them for the good they're doing. Provide addresses, fax numbers and e-mail addresses. Send kind letters to other people who serve your community. Supply sisters with nice stationery or have them make their own that night.

"HOLDING HANDS AND HEARTS"

Contact local churches to find out how you can combine efforts to meet the needs of people in your community. Invite leaders from other religions to speak to your sisters about their faith and what they're doing to improve the community.

"HAPPY HAMMERS"

Help build a Habitat for Humanity House. If sisters can't do physical labor they could provide lunches and snacks for workers or sew curtains. Check out www.habitat.org.

"SIGHT NIGHT" OR
"JEEPERS CREEPERS, WE NEED YOUR OLD PEEPERS!"

Working with Lens Crafters and Lions Club International, collect old prescription glasses that could then be donated to those in need. Check out www.sightnight.org

"A MOTHER'S LOVE"

Find an orphanage to sponsor. There are also homes for wayward teens that could use some motherly love. No doubt they'll have a long list of projects your Relief Society could help with!

"KNITS OF THE ROUND TABLE"

This is a great chance to teach sisters how to knit or crochet and have their creations go to a good cause. Knit or crochet leper bandages for colonies in India. Contact the Church's Humanitarian Department for fabric dimensions and mailing instructions. Learn about how children have helped warm the homeless through their Knits Of The Round Table project.

"WOMEN'S SHELTER"

Gather items for an abused women's shelter. Make curtains or tablecloths to brighten the home or create toiletry kits for the women to keep. Because of security issues, your sisters will probably not be allowed to go inside the home but there is much good they can do to help ease the suffering of the women who temporarily live there.

"BACK TO SCHOOL"

Create school kits to donate to low-income children. Bags could include school supplies and personal items.

"TOYS FOR TOTS"

Gather and clean toys to donate to children in need. Check out www.toysfortots.org. Have sisters bring their children's old, ragged dolls and stuffed animals and have a toy workshop to repair and refresh them. If children have outgrown toys they could be donated to your church's nursery or a local children's group.

"SOUP'S ON!"

Serve at a soup kitchen together one night!

"YOU CAN MAKE A DIFFERENCE"

Contact the Church's Humanitarian Department for ideas on performing dozens of service projects. Either call (801) 240-6060 or e-mail HumanitarianCenter@ldschurch.org. You can also check out www.lds.org/ldsfoundation/welfare. Find out how you can help with the upcoming EFY service projects to be held in your area during the summer.

"ANGELS AMONG US"

Call Deseret Industries, The Salvation Army, Goodwill, United Way, The Kidney Foundation, or other local organizations to give you ideas of service projects you can do as a group that would benefit people in your community. Invite spokesmen from service organizations to tell you how to help in your own community.

"HELP WANTED"

Check out national service organizations that often have projects perfect for Enrichment Night such as The Happy Factory, Care Wear, Crafting Angels, Project Linus, Newborns in Need, Locks of Love, etc. There are so many ways to help!

SERVICE IN CHURCH

"THE TASTE OF SERVICE"

Share ideas on how your kitchen can bless others. Pass around a calendar to have sisters take turns bringing in meals for the busy Bishopric when they start doing Tithing Settlement appointments in November and December. If you don't have one already, pass around another sign-up sheet for sisters to make dinner appointments for the full-time missionaries. Offer to make sack lunches for all of the missionaries on transfer day or Zone Conference.

"BABY SHOWER"

Gather and clean toys for the nursery at church. Serve pink and blue refreshments, and decorate with baby and toddler décor.

"YOU CAN DO IT"

Plan to have sisters help out with a Cannery or Bishop's Storehouse assignment.

"LENGTHEN YOUR STRIDE"

Discuss how to magnify your calling. Invite leaders from all of the church auxiliaries to share what their programs are about and what goals they have for their service. Help sisters understand that *how* they serve is more important than *where* they serve and that their attitude of service is a reflection of their feelings of the Savior.

"THE DOOR TO A BISHOP'S HEART"

Decorate the Bishop's door with thank you letters, pictures of families in the ward, or other fun items that remind him he is loved and appreciated.

"BLACK NAME TAG"

Adopt a missionary. Call the mission home in your area to find out if there are any missionaries who aren't receiving emotional support from their families and offer to send them letters of encouragement or care packages of love.

"SWEET GRATITUDE" OR
"AN ATTITUDE OF GRATITUDE"

Make candy bouquets to give to members of your Ward Council or other auxiliary leaders. Show sisters how to make cookie bouquets and other creative confections to give as thank you gifts to children's teachers, your mailman, friends, home teachers, etc. Help sisters know how to teach their children gratitude and generosity.

"HAVE SMILE, WILL TRAVEL"

Divide the sisters into small groups that could visit other sisters who are in the hospital, in nursing homes, or unable to attend Enrichment Night. Be sure to coordinate plans with the Relief Society Presidency and the sisters you want to visit ahead of time.

"AS SISTERS IN ZION" OR "THE LORD'S HANDS"

Set up tables so the sisters can make cute cards or stationery they can give to the sisters they visit teach. Present new craft techniques for cards such as stamping, gold embossing, using pressed flowers, etc. Make one of those cute refrigerator magnets that says "Visiting Teaching" and a sign that says "Done" on one side and "Not Done Yet" on the other to remind sisters to complete their assignments on time. Have the sisters make "calling cards" with their phone numbers on them that they can give out to the sisters they visit teach.

"SOLD" OR "WELCOME HOME"

Put together "Starter Kits" that the Relief Society presidency can deliver to new sisters moving into your ward. Provide a list of important phone numbers, your ward directory, a city map, local newspaper, library events, bus schedule, etc.

"THE LORD'S HOUSEKEEPING"

Clean the Church building. Schedule a night with the Agent Bishop who is in charge of your building facilities. Find out when your nearest temple will be closed for cleaning and how you can volunteer there.

"DON'T EAT THE DAISIES"

Plant flowers outside on the Church grounds. Be sure to get approval first from your Agent Bishop and/or Stake President! You could even coordinate with the Young Women and plant flowers using colors that reinforce the Young Women Values theme.

"INDOOR FLOWER GARDEN"

Learn the basics for flower arranging and make some flower arrangements to decorate the chapel, using fresh or silk plants.

"THE SONG OF THE RIGHTEOUS"

Clean and repair the hymnals in your church building. Talk about the importance of music in Church and in our lives.

"HEART ATTACK"

Have sisters cut out paper hearts and prepare other items to give someone a "heart attack" by anonymously putting hearts all over their car, front yard or bedroom.

"SERVICE SCAVENGER HUNT"

Group sisters together and have them do a scavenger hunt where the items on their list have to be checked off by someone they have served. Items could include reading a book to a child, picking up garbage, cleaning someone's car windows, pulling weeds, vacuuming a room, etc. Give prizes to the quickest and most creative teams. Talk about how sisters can make doing chores at home more fun for themselves and their children by incorporating games into their work.

"CAMP CHAMPS"

Make things to surprise the young women and Boy Scouts when they will be at their camps in the summer. You could make goodie bags, write loving letters of encouragement, design special stationery for them to use that has their theme on it, put together care packages, make special journals or make a festive poster they could hang at their camp site letting them know they are loved by their ward.

Sisters can reminisce about their favorite camp memories, sing camp songs, and have S'mores for dessert.

"SERVICE SWAP"

Encourage sisters to write down something they could do of service for another sister and put the card in a decorated box. Have the sisters then draw out a card to both give and receive a service. Sisters could write down such things as: cut a child's hair, give rides to the temple, baby-sit children, make a batch of cookies, cook dinner, give a massage, etc. You could spice up the sharing by playing a "White Elephant" game with these cards where the sisters take turns either drawing out a new card or "stealing" a desired service card from another sister.

"DIRTY WORK" OR "DIRTY HARRIET"

Have all sisters wear their grubby clothes and go paint a fence, mow a lawn, weed a garden, or clean the house of a sister in need. If you can't think of anyone who needs help, come to my house!

"KITCHEN CLEAN-UP"

Have the sisters clean up the kitchen in your ward building. Make dish towels for your ward kitchen. Put labels on cabinets to organize shelves and identify a Lost And Found area.

"THE VOICE OF ANGELS"

Have the sisters take turns reading books aloud and record them on tape to loan to sisters who have poor eyesight and can't read any more or who spend a lot of time in their cars and could listen to the book while they drive. You could also have a corner each month during Enrichment where sisters would spend a few minutes recording the Ensign or other church magazines on to cassette to share with others.

"RISE AND SHINE"

Prepare goodies and notes for the Seminary students that meet in your building.

"THE MARK OF A GOOD WOMAN"

Provide a room where sisters can mark certain scriptures in new copies of the Book of Mormon that the missionaries can give to their investigators. Have music playing or even a recording of the scriptures on cassette that the sisters can listen to while they work. You could take a digital picture of each sister and print it out that night to place on a special page inserted in the front of the scriptures with each sister's written testimony.

CHAPTER TEN

Physical And Emotional Health

D&C 10:4 "Do not run faster or labor more than you have strength and means provided to enable you to translate; but be diligent unto the end."

Mosiah 4:27 "And see that all these things are done in wisdom and order; for it is not requisite that a man should run faster than he has strength. And again, it is expedient that he should be diligent, that thereby he might win the prize; therefore, all things must be done in order."

EXERCISE AND NUTRITION

"PARTY LIKE IT'S 1999"

Have someone teach a class about how to celebrate the New Year alcohol-free. The class could include yummy drink recipes, how to make fun party hats, and tips on how to keep all ages entertained until that ball drops in New York Square. Talk about New Year's resolutions and how to improve your health and fitness for the new year.

"BIKER BABES"

Learn how to do easy bicycle repair for your children's bikes and yours. Invite a local sponsored team to talk about how women and their families can get involved in community bike races, clubs, and other biking events. Share tips on good places to go on bike rides in your area for a workout or for fun with the family. Show different kinds of helmets and talk about bike safety.

"BEACH PARTY"

Decorate the cultural hall like a beach and play volleyball inside. Tell the women to wear comfortable clothing they can move in. Model beach-type clothes to get in the mood. Use cute beach decorations and serve drinks with umbrellas in them. If you live near the ocean you could offer classes in how to surf as well as care for surfboards and boogie boards, keeping your skin safe in the summer sun, rip tides, ocean safety and lifeguard skills.

"YOGA"

Have a real yoga teacher show the sisters different kinds of stretches and positions to improve flexibility and strength. Remind the women to wear comfortable clothing they can move around in. Introduce the sisters to Pilates workouts and other low-impact movement workouts.

"BUST A MOVE"

Invite an aerobics instructor to teach a fun class and talk about different kinds of aerobic exercise from Step classes to Tae Bo to dance to good old-fashioned "Richard Simmons" style.

"H$_2$O" OR "AQUA AEROBICS"

If someone in your ward has a pool and doesn't mind hosting an Enrichment Night at their house it would be great fun to offer an Aqua Aerobics class! Invite a teacher from a local sporting club or fitness center to lead the ladies in a class. Show the women different kinds of equipment they could use to increase resistance and add variety.

"AEROBIC INTERVAL TRAINING"

Talk about what aerobic means (with oxygen) and interval training (high-intensity intermittent exercise). Discuss different kinds of training such as Kick boxing, Spinning, Resistance balls, and lifting weights.

"KINESIOLOGY 101"

Invite a personal trainer to teach the sisters the basics on lifting weights and shaping their muscles. Talk about muscle groups, body sculpting, workout tips, and fat loss. Teach the women a few routines they can do with small hand weights.

"BUNS OF STEEL"

Have a review of popular workout videos and form a club for women who are interested in swapping their videos for variety.

"SAFE SWEAT"

Invite a Martial Arts instructor to teach the sisters about personal safety, but also give them a real class so they can see what a great workout it can be!

"FANCY FOOTWORK"

Learn about footwear for different sports and how to choose the right shoe. Talk about athletic shoes for your family and discuss creative ways to deal with children who think they can't live without the most expensive sports shoes.

"COUCH POTATO"

Offer tips for women who have couch potatoes living in their homes and how to get them moving again. Talk about childhood obesity and how to get children interested in sports programs. Discuss TV snacking and offer healthy alternatives.

(SEE "HEALTH AND HYGIENE" ON PAGE 121)

"HERE WE GO AGAIN" OR "YO-YO DIETING"

Invite a nutritionist to discuss healthy eating, fad diets, the Word of Wisdom, and how to lose weight in a safe way. Talk about dieting for children.

"EATING DISORDERS"

This class offers help and healing for sisters who suffer from eating disorders or have loved ones who struggle with anorexia, bulimia, or compulsive overeating.

"NUTRITION NAVIGATION"

Discuss health and nutrition sites on the Internet and how to tell the difference between fact and fiction. Help sisters learn how to research health issues and find answers to their medical questions.

"AH SUGAR, SUGAR" OR "SWEET NOTHINGS"

Find a health educator or someone who teaches Diabetes education classes to share information and ideas about sugar free foods, blood sugar levels and insulin, diabetes prevention and diagnosis. Sample sugar substitutes and discuss the dangers of certain chemicals used in diet foods.

STRESS MANAGEMENT AND RECREATION

"THE WRITE THERAPY" OR "THE JOY OF JOURNALS"

Discuss the power of writing for growth and healing. Talk about different kinds of journals that focus on a particular theme such as gratitude, spirituality, humor, anger control or love. Sisters could decorate a new journal to get them excited about starting to write again.

"TAI CHI FOR HEALTH AND RELAXATION"

Introduce the sisters to this ancient form of meditation and relaxation. Have the ladies wear comfortable clothing to practice some of the moves.

"I COULD HAVE DANCED ALL NIGHT"

There are so many fun styles of dance that you could offer an entire Enrichment Evening with mini-classes teaching ballroom and Latin dance styles, modern, ballet, tap, jazz, hip hop, country line dance and more!

"IN AND OUT"

No, I'm not talking about the famous burger chain started in southern California...I'm talking about a class that teaches breathing and relaxation techniques to control pain, reduce anxiety, slow vital signs, and relieve stress and tension. Find a teacher at a local hospital or health center who can teach the sisters some of the many deep breathing techniques and relaxation exercises.

"GOODBYE TO SHY"

This class will help you learn how to reduce anxiety, build self-esteem, strike up conversations with others, win friends, and act confidently in romantic relationships.

"MMMMMM"

Sisters will enjoy this relaxing class as they learn about the healing qualities of essential oils, the properties of scent and their uses in bath, massage and ambiance. Talk about aromatherapy and show how they can use scented oils, candles, potpourri, incense, and cooking to enhance the smells and moods in their own homes.

"RUB A DUB DUB"

Teach sisters how to make pretty bath salts, body scrubs, sprays, and oils to turn bath time into rejuvenation time. Learn how to turn your bedroom into a sanctuary or create another space in your home that helps you relax and find time for quiet reflection. You could also teach moms how to make inexpensive bubble bath for their children and make bath time fun for dirty toddlers.

"POOL PARTY"

Most sisters will feel self-conscious getting into a bathing suit around each other so you could have a mock pool party in your church building, using cute pool decorations and one of those plastic kiddie pools filled with beach balls or refreshments. Talk about how to find the perfect bathing suit to fit your body type and display lots of modest styles. Discuss SPF and how to protect skin while outside in the summer time and all year round. Share ideas for fun pool games.

"TRAVEL TIPS"

Invite a travel agent to share tips on planning the perfect vacation for a couple's getaway or family trip. Talk about on-line travel resources, traveling with children, trip insurance, tourist traps, all-inclusive resorts, and how to save money on hotel, plane, and car rentals. Anticipation is half the fun you know.

"LAST COMIC STANDING"

This light-hearted class helps sisters see the joy in every day life and the importance of being able to laugh at ourselves and not take everything so seriously. Teach sisters how to create a "Humor Journal" for themselves and their families and how to use one to record and remember the funny things people say and do. They say a good laugh is like a jog around the track.

"WHEN ONLY CHOCOLATE WILL DO"

This lighthearted class helps women learn about and understand PMS. Offer tools to control wacky hormones and mood swings. Sample lots of chocolate. Discuss women's health, menopause, and how to deal with stress without ripping your husband's head off once a month. Talk about ways to deal with stress other than using food.

"HOBBIES THAT COMBAT INSANITY"
Discuss the importance of stress-relieving hobbies and have sisters share what they do to relax and get their creative juices flowing again.

"AN APPLE A DAY"
Invite a nutritionist to talk about healthy lifestyles. Read the Word of Wisdom and discuss changes in your diet that correspond to its counsel. You could tie other classes into this theme by serving apple pie or apple crisp, making cute teacher gifts with apple motif, etc.

"SWEATIN' WITH THE OLDIES"
Have an exercise video swap. Have a review of a variety of exercise tapes or sisters could talk about which ones they like and dislike. Show short clips from the videos and have sisters try different kinds of workouts.

"RELIEF SOCIETY OLYMPICS"
To get the sisters moving their bodies in a fun, less threatening way you could arrange stations that the sisters rotate through. Highlight a few sisters doing a funny competition such as balloon volleyball, finger gymnastics, or bowling with plastic milk cartons. Pretend

gold medals could be passed out to all participants. Decorate with flags from different countries and lots of gold rings made out of paper or cardboard and painted the appropriate colors. Don't forget a pretend Olympic torch! Play national anthems from different countries. Have someone welcome all of the sisters in French and invite a local performing group to create an "Opening Ceremony" show. If you're lucky enough to have a former Olympian living in the area, invite him/her to share some of his experiences.

"SCALING DOWN"

Invite someone who knows a lot about weight management to talk about fad diets, insulin levels, metabolism, and how to lose weight the smart way. Teach the women how to use a fat caliper to calculate body composition. Show different kinds of scales that measure body fat as well as pounds. Be very sensitive to sisters who are struggling with a lot of weight. Invite sisters to share their experiences with weight loss clinics such as Weight Watchers, Over Eaters Anonymous, Jenny Craig, Atkins, etc.

"DEATH BY CHOCOLATE"

This class might include how to make chocolate dipped treats, chocolate fondue, how to find comfort without food, other decadent desserts, and why exactly it is that women respond psychologically and physically to the magical cocoa bean!

"DE-STRESS NIGHT" OR "PAMPER NIGHT"

My ward does this every year and the sisters LOVE this! They never want to go home at the end of the evening! We decorate the

Cultural Hall with pink tablecloths and flowers so it looks like a real feminine spa. You could also decorate with a relaxing Japanese motif using lots of natural materials like bamboo, rocks, and water fountains. Each sister gets to pick her first station and can then rotate to the other ones if time allows. Refreshments could include healthy things like fruits & veggies with dip or else you could serve something terribly decadent and make the sisters feel really spoiled. Choices for stations could include: Manicure, Pedicure, Hot wax on hands, feet and elbows, Facial massage, Make-up tricks and tips, Eyebrow shaping, Skin care, and Posture.

"DREAM TEAM"

Create a Relief Society sports team for basketball, volleyball or any other sport the sisters are interested in. Hold practices and invite another ward to play you.

"MAN'S BEST FRIEND"

While some say that having to take care of an animal adds more stress to an already busy life, most people will recognize that petting a family dog or cat is very relaxing and aids in stress management. Talk about pet care, choosing the right pet and breed, and service projects you can do with your pet such as taking it to a retirement home so the residents can enjoy a visit with Fido.

FEELING GRATITUDE AND RECOGNIZING THE LORD'S BLESSINGS

"GRACIOUS GRATITUDE"

Make thank you cards using clever play on words and attaching coordinating items to them such as "Thanks for being a SOUPer friend!," "I could BEARly have made it without your help," "Without sound too CORNy I wanted to thank you," etc. Have sisters use them for their families, visiting teaching, and children's teachers. Talk about the importance of giving thanks all year long, not just during Thanksgiving.

"SPOUSE APPRECIATION"

Would you believe there are web sites with tons of ideas on how to show appreciation to your hubby? Share ideas with the sisters and send them home excited about putting the spark back into their marriage. Provide a craft table so the women could write love letters to their husbands or children.

"AMERICAN APPRECIATION" OR "OPERATION APPRECIATION"

Set out a table with patriotic stationery, cards and stickers for sisters to write letters of thanks and encouragement to military men and women serving overseas. Put together care packages and even a video greeting from the Relief Society.

"YOU ARE SPECIAL"

Teach sisters how to make those red "You Are Special" plates by inviting a ceramics instructor to lead the workshop. You could also make "You Are Special" placemats, napkins, doorknob hangers, or other items to use when you want to mark a special occasion or acknowledge someone's achievements.

"SWEET NOTHINGS"

Show the sisters how to make candy grams for their families using candy bars on a poster to replace certain words in a loving letter. Share other ideas for using store bought candies to leave loving mementos for family members.

"CHRISTMAS CRAFTS"

Offer a class that focuses on gifts your children can make for Christmas, birthday or other giving occasions.

"THE APPLE OF MY EYE"

Share ideas for great teachers' gifts, children's thank you cards to Primary teachers or scout leaders, coaches, etc. Help mothers know how to teach their children gratitude and generosity.

"A DOSE OF MORTALITY"

Take sisters on a field trip to a cemetery or mortuary to remind them how precious and fleeting this life is. Talk about how to make funeral plans for a loved one and the importance of wills and other estate documents.

"THANKS IN DEED"

Have sisters write letters to their local Congressmen, media, and school boards to thank them for the good they're doing. Provide addresses, fax numbers and e-mail addresses. Supply stationery or have the sisters learn how to design their own.

"FINDING JOY IN EVERY DAY LIFE" OR "THE PURSUIT OF HAPPINESS"

What busy mother doesn't need this refresher course? Help women to seek out moments of joy and happiness in between washing dishes, changing diapers, cooking, and cleaning every day. Talk about the difference between happiness and joy and how to keep an eternal perspective when you're knee deep in laundry.

"LEARNING TO LOVE YOURSELF" OR "WARM FUZZIES"

This class helps sisters to gain a greater love and appreciation for themselves and all of the good they are doing. Offer ways to improve self-esteem and feelings of self-worth. Discuss confidence-building exercises, hormones, and other techniques to improve mental health.

"DAILY DOSE"

Have sisters decorate a mason jar with a padded top and cute ribbons. Cut up 365 slips of paper prepared with written uplifting thoughts—one for each day of the new year. Talk about using positive affirmations, exercise and healthy foods to improve attitude and feel gratitude for what we have.

"QUEENS AND CROWNS"

Invite the Young Women leaders and/or some of the girls to talk about their Young Women Value entitled "Divine Nature." They will have a lot of ideas for classes, activities, decorations, and crafts that reinforce individual worth and self esteem. This could be a great opportunity to host a Mother/Daughter Enrichment Evening.

"ATTITUDE OF GRATITUDE"

Create a "Gratitude Journal" using cute craft techniques the sisters are interested in learning. Talk about the importance of attitude in feeling grateful for our blessings.

"FLOWERFUL THANKS"

Have sisters learn how to make boutonnieres for weddings and to give to fathers on Father's Day at church. Show sisters how to do flower arranging. You could even have the women sign up to take turns making flower arrangements to use in the chapel each week. Show other ways to create "flowerful thanks" using other kinds of materials from your backyard or garden. Teach sisters how to make bouquets out of cookies, fruit, candy, family photos or other creative items.

CHAPTER ELEVEN

Personal Development and Education

D&C 88:118 "And as all have not faith, seek ye diligently and teach one another words of wisdom; yea, seek ye out of the best books words of wisdom; seek learning, even by study and also by faith.

D&C 130:18-19 "Whatever principle of intelligence we attain unto in this life, it will rise with us in the resurrection."

PATRIARCHAL BLESSINGS

"AN EVENING WITH THE PATRIARCH"

Invite your Stake Patriarch to talk about patriarchal blessings and to share some of his experiences while serving the people in your area. Invite his wife to share her insights and talk about experiences she has had while helping her husband. Talk about other patriarchs in the scriptures as well as other blessings that are recorded in the Bible.

"THE ABRAHAMIC COVENANT"

Discuss the importance of the Abrahamic Covenant and its application in the latter days. Help sisters understand the tribes of Israel and their spiritual lineage. Talk about the responsibilities and blessings of Ephraim and Manasseh.

"TIME CAPSULE"

Teach sisters how to create a personal or family time capsule. Have sisters write a letter to themselves in the future, describing what kind of woman they hope to be.

"PATRIARCH PACKET"

Prepare a Family Home Evening packet that mothers can use with their families to teach children about patriarchal blessings and how to spiritually prepare to receive their own some day.

DEVELOPING TALENTS AND CREATIVITY

"A NEW YOU"

Talk about setting realistic, yet challenging goals to stretch yourself. Discuss how to make New Years resolutions that will actually be kept throughout the year and how to include goals that inspire creativity and develop talents. Talk about setting goals in different areas such as physical, spiritual, intellectual, emotional and social. Share insights and even clips from books on tapes by popular motivational speakers such as Steven R. Covey, Anthony Robbins, or Zig Ziglar. Provide web sites to helpful personal coaches.

"YOU TAKE THE CAKE"

Teach the women how to decorate cakes, using creative techniques for all occasions. Have the sisters decorate a cake for the refreshments for the evening or one they can each take home to share with their families. To cut expenses, sisters interested in attending this class could bring a cake they have baked at home to decorate during the class. You could also have them practice different techniques on small cupcakes.

"IT'S SEW EASY!"

Learn different sewing techniques such as how to sew an item with pleats or cording, how to sew on snaps and zippers, making buttonholes, how to sew ribbing or bias tape on fabric, etc.

"CREATIVE CANVAS" OR "FOOT ART"

Learn how to design and make floor cloths for your home. You could also create wall hangings and table runners using the same hand-painted techniques and materials.

"PATTERN SWAP"

If you have a lot of sisters who are interested in sewing you could host a "Pattern Swap" where sisters exchange sewing patterns. Have someone teach the sisters how to adjust patterns for sizes and different kinds of fabrics.

"SUGAR AND SPICE AND EVERYTHING NICE"

This title could describe any crafting class that makes cute things for little girls such as hair bows, dress up socks and shoes, how to do hair braids and other cool hairdos, doll making, etc. This would be a great class to offer before Christmas so moms could make gifts or later in the year for a special Mother/Daughter Enrichment Night.

"TWAS THE NIGHT BEFORE CHRISTMAS"

Make Christmas tree skirts, stockings, advent calendars, Nativity sets out of wood, ornaments and other décor for this special time of year. Avoid the commercial images of Christmas and remember the reason for the season!

"OLE' PAPER MACHE"

Teach the women how to make their own Pinatas, Easter eggs, and other items using paper mache. Invite sisters from a nearby Spanish branch to share some of their other fun customs with you.

"SANTA'S WORKSHOP"

Before Christmas have the sisters get their glue guns, needle and thread ready to repair toys to donate to shelters, orphanages, and hospitals.

"SWEET SHOPPE"

Make lollipops, candy and confections. This is a great class to offer right before the holiday season starts for gift ideas and holiday entertaining. There are even some cool molds of temples and other miscellaneous LDS shapes. If you can't find those you can create your own molds!

"RAG RUGS"

Show the women how to use their old fabric scraps to create rag rugs and other items to give as gifts and decorate their homes. Talk about other discarded materials that could be used for other projects to encourage thrift and ingenuity.

"SISTERS SHOWCASE"

Feature musical talent by the sisters in your ward. Showcase them during a special talent show or as entertainment during an Enrichment dinner.

"THE GREAT COVER UP" OR "SUPER SLIP UPS"

Teach the women how to do a quick and easy makeover for their furniture by making slipcovers and decorative pillows. Show them how to update and care for upholstery items and tapestries. Encourage sisters to beautify their homes and show them how they can do it without spending a fortune.

"FAUX PAS"

Learn how to marbelize old bowls, candlesticks, and decorative pieces at home for a fresh, new look. Show sisters how to use old items to create new looks and beautify their homes.

""FAR ABOVE RUBIES"

Learn how to make jewelry. Remind the sisters that a virtuous women's price is far above rubies. Offer to make some for the Young Women by using colored stones that coordinate with their themed values.

"VIP TREATMENT"

Make your family feel like VIP's in your own home by learning how to make beautiful, yet inexpensive window treatments. Talk about different kinds of curtains, cornice boxes, valances, and draperies. Show pictures of creative wall treatments using clever substitutes for hardware such as fishing poles, golf clubs, tree branches and pool cubes. (I know that may sound strange, but it's all the rage with interior designers these days.)

"GUESS WHO'S COMING TO DINNER"

Show sisters how to make placemats, napkins, napkin rings, and place settings for their seasonal tables as well as when they invite other families over for dinner.

"BLOOMING BULBS"

Learn how to plant and grow forced bulbs such as Narcissus, tulips, hyacinths, etc. during the winter months. To give as Christmas gifts you'll need to start in September. Be sure to talk about the glory of nature and the blessings of Heavenly Father's creative hands.

"PROUD TO BE AN AMERICAN"

Make patriotic decorations for home and yard in honor of the many patriotic occasions during the year (Flag Day, Veteran's Day, Independence Day, Memorial Day, Labor Day). Talk about what a blessing it is to live where you do.

"ROSES ARE RED, VIOLETS ARE BLUE"

Learn how to write different kinds of poetry. Teach the sisters about different styles and share passages from famous poets throughout history. Encourage the sisters to write and give awards for the "Most Romantic," "Most Creative," "Funniest," etc.

"MAGAZINE MANIA"

Learn how to write articles to submit to the Church magazines. Find out what the submission guidelines are. Send in a picture and story of something your Relief Society has done that is especially inspiring. If you have a group of interested writers in your ward you could also talk about how to submit freelance stories to other magazines.

"DON'T BURY YOUR TALENTS"

Do a talent exchange where each sister writes something she can do for another sister on a 3x5 card and puts it in a specially decorated box where other sisters have added their cards. The women can randomly draw a card that shows something they will receive from another sister or else all of the cards could be openly displayed and sisters choose which card they would like. Provide a deadline and follow-up event when experiences can be shared. "Talents" could be simple things such as baking bread, sewing something, teaching piano lessons, babysitting, taking a family photo, etc. Remind the sisters that everyone has something wonderful to offer.

"I'VE BEEN FRAMED"

Show how to frame and mat pictures professionally but inexpensively. Invite a local frame shop to show you techniques and provide equipment. Create special frames to display family photos, "The Proclamation To The World," or temples. You could also make a special frame with a slot that opens at the top so a different picture could be displayed each week for Family Home Evening, using the Church's artwork collection or the pictures inside the monthly Ensign magazine.

"WRITE ON"

Find an English teacher or a sister who writes especially well to teach the sisters how to write more effectively. Sisters could share their creative stories with each other and silly prizes could be awarded such as "The story that made us laugh the hardest" or "Best tear-jerker story" or "Most likely to turn into a made for TV movie." Show sisters how to use creative writing styles for their annual Christmas family letter and even in their journals.

"BUILD A BEAR"

Teach sisters how to sew and create their own stuffed animals for gifts, to donate to needy children, or to create heirloom items for their families.

(SEE THE "CULTURAL ARTS" CHAPTER STARTING ON PAGE 193 FOR OTHER IDEAS ON TALENTS FOR MUSIC, ART, DANCE AND OTHER CREATIVE ARTS)

LIFELONG LEARNING

"THE ELUSIVE BRASS RING" OR "COLLEGE DROP OUT NO MORE"

Encourage sisters who once started their college degrees to learn how they can still earn their diploma. Teach them about Independent Study programs, On-line degrees, and distance education. Talk about time management, tuition, financial aid and the importance of accreditation when choosing a school.

"CAMPUS CRUSADE"

Invite sisters who have attended some of BYU's wonderful educational events and camps to share their experiences. Check out www.byu.edu for more information about BYU Education Week, Women's Conference, Know Your Religion, and Families Under Fire. (Click on "Continuing Education.")

"TIME OUT FOR WOMEN"

If you're lucky enough to have one of these events in your area, encourage your sisters to attend! Consider forming a Time Out Book Club in your ward as well to earn free books for your sisters. Check out www.deseretbook.com/time-out.

"POWER POINT"

Teach the sisters how to create Power Point presentations they can use for family reunions, Family Home Evening, business, Girls Camp, church lessons, or any occasion!

"SEASONED SISTERS" OR "CULINARY SCHOOL 101"

Invite a local chef or someone who teaches at a cooking school to teach his/her specialty. Have a pastry chef teach the women how to prepare finger desserts for a special event such as an Eagle Court of Honor, Young Women's "New Beginnings," Women's Conference, etc.

"CHARLOTTE'S WEB" OR "WONDER WEB WOMAN"

Show the sisters how to design a Web page, how to register a domain name to create a family web site or one for a home business, web space, ISP, and other tips for establishing one's own web address.

"CYBER MAMA"

Find a friendly computer geek to teach the sisters all about word processing, spreadsheets, data bases, and other computer applications that they can use to help them with their callings, family history, Family Home Evening preparation, home businesses, etc.

"PERPETUAL EDUCATION FUND"

Invite someone who has been on the receiving end of the Church's Perpetual Education Fund to share his/her feelings and experiences. Talk about what the sisters can do to reach out and help others attain their education.

"THE POLITICAL PARTY" OR "PARTY WITH POLITICS"

Invite one of your Congressmen, City Councilmen, a high school government teacher, or someone who works with your local government to offer a refresher course on how laws are made, how government works, and how everyone can make a difference. Use your discretion on whom you invite, as campaigning is not allowed in the church buildings. Talk about current events and what the sisters can do to have their voices heard about important legislation.

"THE ETERNAL STUDENT"

Invite a teacher or administrator from a community college to talk about what courses are available or to share a sample lesson from one of the classes. Encourage sisters to develop one of their talents or find a new hobby that will enrich their lives by attending a community college course. Discuss which adult education classes are held at night on nearby high school campuses.

"THE CREATION"

This idea has been popular in Relief Society for years and involves using a theme for mini-classes that follow the seven days of the world's creation: **Day 1**: Organizing matters in your home, goals, time management. **Day 2**: Water safety, water sports, laundry, bath time fun for kids. **Day 3**: Decorating with lights (up-lights, spotlights, recessed lights, etc), make cute night-lights for children's rooms. **Day 4**: Yard work, gardening, landscaping ideas, and weed control. **Day 5**: Animal care, Choosing pets, Selecting dog breeds, Salt-water fish tanks. **Day 6**: Improving marriage & relationships, communication, obedience. **Day 7**: How to keep the Sabbath Day holy, spiritual & physical renewal, relaxation techniques.

"RED, WHITE AND BLUE"

Classes offered during this patriotic-themed night could include making patriotic pins or T-shirts, clever ideas how to decorate a bike or wagon for a parade, understanding how your local government works, meet and greet local politicians, special patriotic musical numbers, and a Reader's Theatre where sisters read quotes from famous Americans.

"READING MATTERS"

Have a Book review. This could be an entire class or even just a five-minute presentation each month by a sister who has read a particular book and gives a quick review about it, encouraging other sisters to read it in the future. Talk about BYU Honor's list of fine literature. Invite a local librarian to share highlights from some of the popular books.

"TIC TOC"

Share ideas for time management and help sisters learn how to organize their lives and families. Teach skills that will help them with the rest of their lives by setting long-range goals, weekly task lists, family calendar tips, and personal planning. Offer creative ideas they can use to teach their children the same skills.

"A WOMAN'S WORK" OR "BRINGING HOME THE BACON"

Offer a class for women in the workplace to find balance in their lives. Help them feel supported in their efforts, especially if they are single moms trying to do it all. Talk about helpful resources in and out of the church, job burnout, the importance of time management and health.

"BUY THE BOOK"

Begin a book club. It could be held as part of Enrichment Night or those sisters who are interested could decide another time and place to gather and discuss books of their choosing. Find out which sisters, if any, follow the Oprah Winfrey book club or any of the other book clubs on TV. Those sisters could present some of the books they enjoyed the most and do a review of the next book.

"THE PAPER CHASE"

Have a book swap. For every book someone brings that night to put in a designated box, they get to pick out another book to take home. You could have a separate swap for books on cassette or even one for videos and DVDs.

"COMPUTER NERDS UNITE"

Invite a friendly computer geek to share simple computer repair tips. Talk about the proper care of hardware and software and how to clean the mustard stain out of the keyboard.

"LDS LIBRARY" OR "THE BEEHIVE BOOKSHELF"

Invite someone from your local LDS bookstore to speak to the sisters about their best-selling books. If you're lucky, have a local author share tidbits from his/her latest book. Ask your ward building librarian to share the contents of your church library.

"RAPID READER" OR "QUICKEN THE BRAIN"

Offer a class in speed-reading. Discuss ways to improve comprehension and compare different methods to improve speed.

"BOOK WORM" OR "DOG EARED DELIGHTS"

Invite a mainstream bookstore to talk about some of its best books. They might even bring you some free gift certificates, free bookmarks or coupons if you ask.

"SPEAK EASY"

Have someone from your local Toastmaster's Club make a presentation to the sisters about public speaking, common mistakes, various speaking styles, how to overcome the fear of speaking in public, attention-grabbers, etc. Share tips on how to write good sacrament meeting talks.

"TALKING GOOD"

(You know that's incorrect, right?) Encourage sisters to improve their vocabulary by learning one new word a day. Have an English teacher offer a refresher course on English grammar.

CHAPTER TWELVE

Literacy

Daniel 1:17 "As for these four children, God gave them knowledge and skill in all learning and wisdom: and Daniel had understanding in all visions and dreams."

Moses 6:5-6 "And a book of remembrance was kept, in the which was recorded, in the language of Adam, for it was given unto as many as called upon God to write by the spirit of inspiration."

GOSPEL LITERACY

"LATTER DAY LEGISLATURE"

Become literate about legislation affecting gospel values such as marriage, family, religious symbols on federal property, etc. Talk about what the sisters can do to have their voices heard and how they can get involved with others who want to make a positive difference in their communities.

"WHO'S WHO"

Learn about Who's Who in the scriptures so sisters become more familiar with names. There are some great books that list all of the names and where they are found in the standard works, their contributions and what we can learn from them.

"MEET AND GREET"

Have a local LDS author speak to the sisters about his/her book and talk about the process of writing and the experience of getting something published.

"SCRIPTURE SCHOLARSHIP"

Invite a respected scriptorian to share experiences and tips he/she used over the years to memorize scriptures and understand passages. Share information on your local Adult Institute classes or other scripture study groups the sisters could join.

"SEE SISTER SMITH READ"

Introduce sisters to the Church's "Basic Gospel Literacy Course."

"SATURDAY'S WARRIORS"

Talk about prophecies of the last days and the Book of Revelations.

"TALKING TESTIMONY"

Have the sisters take turns reading books aloud and record them on tape to loan to sisters who have poor eyesight and can't read any more or spend a lot of time in their cars and could listen to the book while they drive. You could also have a corner each month during Enrichment where sisters would spend a few minutes recording the

Ensign or other church magazines on to cassette for others. Create a cassette library where sisters could check out books and Church literature on tape. This would be a fun project to involve the youth or even Primary children!

"THE MORMON TRAIL"

Invite someone who has visited Church history sites to share photos, slides, and personal experiences about what occurred there. Give sisters travel information so they can try to make plans to visit those areas with their families.

"URIM AND THUMMIM"

Learn about the Joseph Smith translations and identify what changes were made to scripture.

"PEARLS AND PAPYRUS"

Learn about the history and discovery of the Pearl of Great Price. Talk about what religious documents have been recently discovered in the Middle East, such as the Dead Sea Scrolls.

"CONFERENCE CHAT"

Pull out the November and May copies of the Ensign to discuss the most recent sessions of General conference. See if you can find a running theme the Church leaders were trying to impress upon the saints. Have sisters share highlights from some of the talks. Outline specific goals your Relief Society could work on until the next General Conference.

"MOVERS AND SHAKERS"

Share biographies of early church leaders and Saints. Talk about their religious backgrounds and experiences that helped them endure the trials that occurred during the early days of the restoration of the Church.

"SPECIAL WITNESS"

Choose a book written by a General Authority to discuss.

"ETERNAL FORTUNE MAGAZINE"

Invite your ward Magazine Rep to attend and bring material the sisters can use to subscribe to the various Church magazines. It would be fun to spotlight some of the popular features or articles in The Ensign, The New Era, and The Friend. Someone who subscribes to the Church News could also share some favorite articles or simply introduce the newspaper to sisters who are unfamiliar with it. Give prizes to sisters who can answer trivia questions from last month's issues.

"TALMAGE TALKS"

Review some of the great classic church books written by Elder James E. Talmage such as *Jesus the Christ, The Articles of Faith, The House Of The Lord*, and *The Great Apostasy.*

"FARMS"

Invite a representative from the F.A.R.M.S. organization to discuss some of the recent discoveries about Ancient America they have found and some of their current efforts to locate Book of

Mormon artifacts and evidences. They'll be happy to bring copies of some of their publications and videos. Interesting stuff!

WRITTEN HISTORIES AND TESTIMONIES

"QUMRON QUESTIONS"

Share interesting information about the Dead Sea Scrolls and talk about the current research that is being done. Discuss the LDS perspective on some of the findings, BYU DNA research, and learn about the Center for the Preservation of Ancient Religious Texts. See http://cpart.byu.edu/dss.php

"DO'S AND DOCENTS"

Take a docent tour of a nearby lagoon, historic house, museum or other education site in your area.

"OLD GEEZERS"

Discuss biographies of Church leaders and other inspirational people from the early days of the restoration of the Church.

"RARE CARE"

Learn about rare books and how to care for them. Invite sisters to bring their old books to have them appraised.

"BEYOND THE PEDIGREE CHART"

This class could be about more advanced genealogy techniques or even have a completely different twist to Family History, that of writing personal histories and autobiographies. Share examples of different kinds of biographies and provide a list or cute jar of "writer's block starters" to give sisters ideas of what to write about in their autobiographies. Invite someone from your local genealogy chapter to share ideas and stories.

"A LONG TIME AGO"

Visit some of the older sisters in your Relief Society who may be unable to attend Enrichment Night due to poor health and help them record their stories and life histories on tape cassette or video.

"TALKS FOR TOTS (AND BIG PEOPLE TOO)"

Invite someone to help sisters learn how to prepare a good talk or lesson for church. Share tips for writing talks for Primary and Sacrament meeting.

"HAVING BEEN BORN OF GOODLY PARENTS"

Teach the sisters how to begin writing their autobiography. Show various styles and provide examples of things they might want to include in their writing such as their first date, favorite elementary school teacher, jobs, lessons learned from church teachers, favorite family traditions, etc.

"INTERVIEW ETIQUETTE"

Share ideas on how to graciously interview relatives for information you can use in a family history book, family reunion, or collection of family stories. Discuss how to share genealogy information with non-members.

"TO BE OR NOT TO BE"

Learn about William Shakespeare, read one of his plays, see a movie version of one of his works and learn how to understand old English prose.

"ROSES ARE REDDISH"

Learn about different kinds of poetry and practice writing some. Award prizes for "Most Romantic," "Funniest," "Most Creative," etc. Encourage sisters to write!

"UNCLE WHO?

Offer a class on how to preserve old family photos, papers to use, how to properly label pictures and documents, and how to display them in your homes. Talk about photography as history.

"DEAR FRIEND"

Begin a Pen Pal program with another Relief Society somewhere in the world.

"PIONEER PALS"

Invite someone who has gone on one of the Church's Pioneer treks to share his/her experiences. If you're really ambitious you could plan one for your Relief Society or ward!

"AUDIO GOSPEL" OR "TALKING TESTIMONY"

Have the sisters take turns reading books aloud and record them on tape to loan to sisters who have poor eyesight and can't read any more or spend a lot of time in their cars and could listen to the book while they drive. You could also have a corner each month during

Enrichment where sisters would spend a few minutes recording the Ensign or other church magazines on to cassette for others. Create a cassette library where sisters could check out books and Church literature on tape. This would be a fun project to involve the youth or even Primary children!

"THE MARK OF A GOOD WOMAN"

Provide a room where sisters can mark certain scriptures in new copies of the Book of Mormon that the missionaries can give to their investigators. Have music playing or even a recording of the scriptures on cassette that the sisters can listen to while they work. You could even take a digital picture of each sister and print it out that night to place on a special page inserted in the front of the scriptures with each sister's written testimony.

"THE AUTHOR'S CORNER"

Have a local author speak to the sisters about his/her book and talk about the process of writing and the experience of getting something published. Learn how to write articles to submit to the Church magazines. Find out what the submission guidelines are. Send in a picture of something your Relief Society has done that is especially inspiring.

"THE THRILL OF VICTORY"

The Olympics offer endless opportunities to find inspiring stories. Share reports and tales of triumph and defeat. Watch an event together. Invite a real Olympian to share his/her experiences.

"WOW WOMEN"

This class shares stories from the lives of incredible women throughout history. Relief Society sisters should leave home inspired and motivated to do more with their lives to bless humanity. Talk about women such as Helen Keller, Eve Curie, Oprah, etc.

"GRANDMA'S FEATHER BED"

Discuss genealogy and how to research the stories behind the dates and names. Share inspiring examples and provide lots of resources where sisters can go to learn more about their ancestors' lives.

EARLY CHILDHOOD EDUCATION AND CHILDREN'S LITERACY

"LDS ABC'S"

Offer insights into Home schooling. Discuss the pros and cons of public school, private school, and home schooling.

"HOMEWORK HASSLES"

Talk about ways to encourage learning at home, foods that affect school behavior, positive daily rituals during the school year, public school tips, how to communicate well with your child's teacher and other resources to help your children succeed in school.

"HOOKED ON READING"

Show different techniques moms can use to teach their pre-school children how to read. Schools and libraries have lists of suggested books for beginning readers that you could share with the sisters. Some libraries even let you use a copy of the "Hooked On Phonics" program for free!

"THE CLASSICS"

Spend an evening discussing some of the great classics in literature. Invite a teacher from your local school to talk about which books your children will be reading and how moms can promote discussion at home. Talk about the various literature awards that are given for children's literature and how to identify a good book from one that's not worth the paper it's printed on. For older children, discuss which books help prepare students for the SAT exam and college.

"YOUR DARLING LITTLE ANGEL"

Invite a pediatrician or early childhood educator to help mothers know what healthy developmental markers there are for education and how to tell if your child is a genius (of course he is) or needs a little extra help academically.

"BOOK SMART"

Have a children's book review. This could be a five-minute presentation each month by a sister who would like to recommend a children's book. A book review could also be a class where one or many books are discussed. Have a book swap. For every book someone brings that night to put in a designated box, they get to pick out another book to take home. You could have a separate swap for books on cassette or even videos and DVDs.

"PRECIOUS PAGES"

Collect books to donate to a local library, Boys & Girls Club, Women's Correctional Facility, homeless shelter, or low-income after school organization.

"STORY TIME"

Invite a local librarian or popular storyteller to share her talents with your Relief Society and give tips to moms on how to tell stories and read books in interesting ways that will hold the interest of their children and grandchildren. Find out when the library has story time hours for children and if your community holds a Storyteller's Festival that your family could attend. Make puppets or talk about other items of interest that could be used to bring books to life. Have sisters volunteer to read books at the library during their Story Time hour.

"READ TO SUCCEED"

Teach how to start a "Read To Succeed" program at your children's school. There are companies like Pizza Hut and Six Flags who give prizes when students read a certain number of books each month. You can find some mothers to help coordinate those efforts at your children's school if they don't already exist through your PTA.

"SISTER FRIENDLY"

Some Primaries have a "Sister Friendly" character who visits monthly and talks about the highlights in the Church's Friend magazine. Invite her to share information about the children's magazines and share tips on how to use the publication in your home. You could do the same thing for teenagers with the New Era magazine. Someone who subscribes to the Church News could also share some favorite articles or simply introduce the newspaper to sisters who are unfamiliar with it and talk about how to get their children interested in reading it.

"BUY THE BOOK"

Invite someone from your local LDS bookstore or mainstream bookstore to speak to the sisters about their best-selling children's books. They'll most likely be happy to bring free bookmarks or other items for moms to share with their children.

"THE SOUND OF SISTERS"

Have the sisters take turns reading children's books aloud and record them on cassette tape to loan to sisters who would like to use them with their children or donate them to the nursery. You could also have a corner each month during Enrichment where sisters would spend a few minutes recording the Friend or other church magazines on to cassette.

"EYE SEE"

Invite an optometrist to teach the sisters how to take care of their children's eyes so they'll have many years of fun reading! The doctor could dispel common myths, talk about different kinds of eyewear and exams, discuss contact lenses for children, and teach what to look for in a good pair of reading glasses that children won't break easily.

"HIDDEN GEMS"

Take a tour of your local library to learn about all of the hidden gems that can be found there! Work with the librarians to register sisters and their children for their own library cards. Find out about special events. You could also create special packets for newborn babies that would include library information and "Baby's First Library Card" and deliver them to your local maternity hospital.

"DOG EARED DELIGHTS"

Spend some time repairing and cleaning the children's books in the nursery in your church building. Collect donated books to add to the children's library. Repair any damaged hymnals in your building as well.

CHAPTER THIRTEEN

Cultural Arts

D&C 25:12 "For my soul delighteth in the song of the heart; yea, the song of the righteous is a prayer unto me, and it shall be answered with a blessing upon their heads."

THE IMPORTANCE OF MUSIC IN THE HOME

"THE SOUND OF MUSIC"

Learn how to conduct music. Show how to make one of those cute visual aids that children use to learn how to conduct music. One example is to create an elephant face out of cardstock and then use a sock to look like the elephant trunk. The child puts his hand in the trunk and moves it around to follow a 2/4, 3/4 or 6/8 music pattern. Talk about what all of the symbols mean on the sheet music and how to change tempo and volume.

"DOE RAY ME"

Form a Relief Society choir that could sing at a special event. Play "Name That Tune" with church hymns and Primary songs.

"KEYS TO MUSIC"

Offer a beginning piano class. Let interested sisters know they can purchase a very inexpensive keyboard and lesson material from the Church Distribution Center. Teach them how to play one hymn on the piano. Share tips on finding a good piano teacher for children.

"THE VOICE OF AN ANGEL"

Have someone give interested sisters an official voice lesson. Learn voice exercises to improve singing.

"1, 2, 3 AND 1, 2, 3 AND…"

Find someone to give sisters an introductory lesson in an instrument such as guitar, piano, flute, spoons, harmonica, etc. Invite a local music store to provide information on local teachers and classes offered in your community.

"A NIGHT AT THE OPERA"

Introduce the sisters to opera by starting with something popular such as "The Phantom Of The Opera" or the "Magic Flute." Invite a singer to perform. Have someone explain the plot of a famous opera. Teach the sisters a few phrases in Italian. Have the sisters wear fancy gowns that night. Make pretend opera glasses out of paper or cardboard that has been spray-painted gold.

"MARCHING BAND AND SWISHING SKIRTS"

Create a Relief Society band or orchestra that could perform at special events.

"DEAR SISTERS DEBUT"

Feature musical talent by sisters in your ward. Showcase them during a special show or as entertainment during an Enrichment dinner.

"BEAUTY SHOP QUARTET"

Invite singers in your ward to present musical numbers every now and then at Enrichment Night. Treat all of the sisters to the musical sounds of the brethren, Primary children, youth and other local musicians. Mix it up with duets, choirs, Barbershop Quartets, solos and instrumental performances.

"AMERICAN IDOL"

Have a talent show. Invite sisters to perform and give everyone a participation award. You could also give complementary awards such as "Most Likely to appear on the David Letterman Show" or "Most likely to be recruited by the Mormon Tabernacle Choir." Be mindful of those sisters who don't feel they have a stage talent to present. Awards for "Most Thoughtful Friend," "Best Muffin Maker," "Best Shoulder To Cry On," for example, could be presented to sisters who have great spiritual talents.

"BEETHOVEN BASICS"

Learn about famous composers. Listen to their styles and have a contest to see who can guess which composer wrote which piece.

FINE ARTS

"PAGEANT OF THE MASTERS"

Find out what cultural events or art festivals occur in your area that showcase uplifting fine arts. Provide calendars and even directions to the sites so sisters can go with their families. Sisters could share their experiences about attending any of those events.

"MEET THE MASTERS"

Introduce the sisters to some of the famous painters throughout history. Learn about their lives and styles. Have a contest to see how many paintings the sisters can identify. Talk about different kinds of art such as watercolor, oils, acrylics, sculpture, pencil and charcoal sketches, printing, etc.

"SHALL WE DANCE?"

Invite a couple who knows how to ballroom dance to perform and then teach the sisters some of the steps to different styles of ballroom or Latin dance such as the Waltz, Cha Cha, Salsa, Tango, Foxtrot, Quickstep, etc.

"CHICK FLICKS"

Have a fun class about movie magic. Talk about film literacy. Learn about camera work, lighting, sound, and special effects. Learn about film history and the development of different genres. Develop a greater appreciation of the people who make movies by understanding production, distribution and piracy. Talk about the current rating system, film censoring companies, and how to choose family-friendly movies for your family to enjoy. Host a "thumbs up" event where a panel of speakers reviews movies. Talk about companies that provide an editing service for rental movies such as "Clean Films."

"GIRLS NIGHT OUT"

Attend local drama productions together for a fun evening. Find out what community theatre events there are or go to support any of the young men and young women in your ward when they perform in their high school productions.

"SWAN SISTERS"

Interview someone from the local ballet company to teach the sisters about the discipline and training involved in putting on a professional ballet production.

There are probably some little girls or teenagers in your ward who are taking ballet lessons who could come and perform and then teach the ladies a few of the moves. During the holidays you could attend "The Nutcracker" together.

"YEEHAW"

Throw a western theme event, complete with decorations, music and line dancing! Have someone teach the sisters a fun dance they can all do together without any men as partners. Invite some sisters or local dancers to perform a country line dance for the group. It would also be fun to have a professional caller come to teach the ladies how to do a hoe down. Decorations could include lots of cow fabric, horse motif, and barn accessories.

UNDERSTANDING OTHER CULTURES

"FELIZ NAVIDAD"

Learn about customs from other cultures that are practiced during Christmas or other holidays. Host an "Around The World" evening where sisters rotate through different stations or rooms that teach about several different countries and holiday celebrations.

"MY GYRO"

Learn about middle-eastern foods and cook a Gyro sandwich. Invite someone to talk about the current political conditions in those countries and how the Church is growing.

"OKTOBERFEST"

October lends itself to hearty food and fun. Hold an Oktoberfest, highlighting German food, dancing, heritage, genealogy, polka, and of course, apple strudel!

"KITCHENS AROUND THE WORLD"

Invite sisters with different ethnic backgrounds to share some of the cooking from their countries.

"LADIES LUAU"

Everyone loves a festive luau and the chance to dream of exotic vacations. It would be fun to give each sister a lei upon entering the room and a traditional Hawaiian kiss on the cheek to welcome them to the island. Classes offered could include Pacific Rim cooking,

Hula dancing, how to play the ukulele, or bathing suit choices for your body type. It would be fun to show slides or display pictures of the Hawaiian temple and even the Polynesian Cultural Center in Oahu. You can get free posters of various Pacific islands at travel agencies to use as wall decorations or give as door prizes. Make miniature palm trees out of cardboard tubes and colored paper.

"THE BEST TWO YEARS"

Have the returned missionaries in your ward share stories, food, pictures, and memorabilia from the countries where they served.

"SHARE YOUR AMERICA"

Learn about how to sponsor a foreign exchange student or safe ways to send your own children abroad through study programs. Check out Rotary Club International for loads of information and for a guest speaker on the ins and outs of student exchange programs and opportunities.

"Sí SENORA"

Offer mini classes in foreign languages such as French, Italian, German, and Spanish. Learn Latin roots for many words. Invite a teacher from a school such as Berlitz to share tips on learning a language quickly and where to take classes.

"MISSION POSSIBLE"

Send each of the sisters on a "mission" to a different country. They could receive a letter in the mail before Enrichment Night, inviting them to attend and telling them where they have been "called" for the evening. Separate rooms can be decorated with items, music and food from selected foreign countries. A speaker could tell them all about that country and how the Church's missionary efforts are going there today. After their time in their "country" they could then rotate through the other countries. Sisters could wear pretend missionary nametags and even be given a companion. Sisters could try to memorize a scripture in a foreign language or try to do a door approach in their new language. A care package from "home" could be given to the sisters with letters from their real family (prepared ahead of time) or simply a love letter from the Relief Society presidency and a treat. You could start everyone off in a pretend "Missionary Training Center" and then send them off to their countries. The mission president from your area could speak to all of sisters about how the work is going. You could invite the real missionaries from your ward to speak as well.

"OLE'"

Invite sisters from a nearby Spanish branch (or another foreign language branch you have in your area) and have them teach the sisters how to prepare traditional dishes from their native country. Teach commonly used phrases and listen to some popular music from their country.

"FLY THE FRIENDLY SKIES"

Decorate one room to look like an airport with travel posters, entry gate, gift shop, newspaper stand, etc. Set up another room to look like an airplane with seats lined up in rows with an aisle in the middle. As the sisters arrive have them check in and receive a boarding pass, seat assignment and passport. Flight attendants could welcome them aboard and serve refreshments. Invite one of the brethren to introduce himself as the captain or tape-record your Bishop's voice to pretend to come from the cockpit. Your airplane could land in various countries or you could have some of the young men in your ward "hijack" the plane and take it to various destinations. You could even have a spy from a certain country come and tell passengers about that country.

"HOLDING HANDS AND HEARTS"

Contact local churches to find out how you can combine efforts to meet the needs of people in your community. This could be a very special evening where women from other religions are invited to share their faith and identify things they have in common with LDS sisters. Help sisters appreciate the good in other religions.

CHAPTER FOURTEEN
Relief Society Birthday Party Ideas

"HISTORY OF RELIEF SOCIETY"

Have someone give a special presentation about the history of the Relief Society in the Church or just in your specific area. Memorabilia and old photos could be displayed.

"RELIEF SOCIETY YEARBOOK"

Begin a Relief Society scrapbook for your ward. Begin taking pictures at each month's meeting that demonstrate what activities and lessons were presented. Take pictures of each of the sisters in your ward and have them write their testimony about Relief Society on a separate page. Each month there could be a scrapbook table set out so sisters could create pages from last month's photos and mementos.

"RELIEF SOCIETY PRESIDENTS"

Learn about all of the former General Relief Society Presidents. Have your ward's Relief Society presidency share a little about themselves to get to know them better. You could also share the history of Relief Society leaders in your ward over the years.

"RELIEF SOCIETY BLESSINGS"

Invite a panel of speakers to share how their lives have been blessed by Relief Society. Panel members could include brethren and children, as well as sisters in your ward.

"DINNER"

Have the young men dress up as waitress, complete with folded towel over their arms, and serve the sisters a special dinner. Brethren from the ward could baby-sit children and provide entertainment while the sisters eat. If you have some really talented musicians in your ward it would be fun to have a strolling violinist or Barbershop Quartet perform from table to table.

"CELEBRATE SISTERHOOD"

Play a lot of icebreaker games where the sisters can really get to know each other. A fun game is when each sister writes on a slip of paper something she has done in her life that is unique. All of the papers are gathered and then read aloud while the group tries to guess who did that thing. The same type of information could be gathered ahead of time and written down on one sheet of paper that each sister is given. She has to write down the name of the person she thinks did that thing and the sister who can guess the most correct answers wins a little prize.

"GET TO KNOW YOU"

Have sisters bring three items that describe themselves, their talents, or hobbies. Items could be set out on a table and sisters would have to guess who brought them and then each woman would take a couple of minutes to identify her objects and talk a little bit about herself. You could also play "The Bean Game:" Everyone sits in a circle and is given a certain number of beans (or whatever item you want to use). Each sister takes a turn telling the group something she has never done in her life that she thinks everyone else in the group has done. Examples could include: "I have never said a bad word," "I have never watched the movie E.T.," "I have never been to SLC," etc. The sisters who HAVE done that thing then have to throw one of their beans into the center pot. If they have NOT done that thing then they get to keep their beans untouched. The winner is the sister who has the most beans at the end of the game.

"QUIZ SHOW"

Turn any popular TV Game show into a Relief Society version. Use questions and answers about Church history, former General and local Relief Society Presidents, ward trivia, scripture characters, and interesting tidbits about your own sisters. Tape record the music from TV to play so everyone really gets into the spirit of the game. Fun TV game shows that work really well are Jeopardy, Hollywood Squares, Wheel of Fortune, Who Wants to Be A Millionaire, and $10,000 Pyramid.

"MORMON BAR"

Here is a bar the sisters can actually go into . . . for refreshments. Set out a long table with all kinds of toppings for a Taco Bar, Potato Bar, or Ice Cream Sundae Bar.

"PAJAMA PARTY"

Have sisters wear modest pajamas and lounge wear and enjoy a fun evening of girl talk, makeup tips, doing each other's hair, bedroom decorating tips, junk food munchies, and even a few innocent games where you wrap each other in toilet paper like mummies or freeze a token bra for old times sake.

"RELIEF SOCIETY IS PRICELESS"

Each table has a decorated jar full of pennies. Sisters take turns picking a penny and then they have to tell something about themselves that happened during that year. If the date is before she was born she has to pick another penny.

"JELLY BEANS"

This is a cute theme to use if Easter occurs near your Relief Society Commemoration party. Each sister picks a jellybean when she enters the room. The color of her jellybean determines which table she will sit at. Tables should be decorated with color-coordinated tablecloths or centerpieces.

"DAY OF SERVICE"

Get back to the basics when Relief Society was first organized by the Prophet Joseph and sisters were called to serve and meet the needs of the poor. Have sisters spend as many hours as they can during a designated day to work on service projects.

"CARNIVAL"

Have booths where sisters have to complete tasks or games to earn prizes. Fun and simple tasks might include answering a Relief Society history quiz, remembering past Enrichment Night activities, Name that Face game using pictures of sisters in your ward, matching temples with locations, or you could even have the sisters come up with clever missionary door approaches to earn prizes. Use gospel twists to traditional carnival games like Bowling, Ring Toss, Bean Bag Toss or Fishing for a Prize. Sisters are given tickets to spend at booths and "buy" refreshments.

"A LAMP UNTO YOUR FEET"

Do a special presentation about the parable of the Ten Virgins. Decorate with small clay lamps. Talk about what sisters need to be and do to join the five wise virgins in being prepared for the Bridegroom's second coming.

"LEADING FAMILIES TO CHRIST"

Center your theme around Sherri L. Dew's statement "We no longer have the luxury of spending our energy on anything that does not lead us and our families to Christ." Discuss ways sisters can focus more on Christ in their homes with their families.

"VALIANT SISTERS"

Share stories and examples of good LDS women in history as well as in the scriptures.

"GARDEN PARTY"

Decorate with flowers, baskets, garden tools, picket fences, clay pots and more flowers! You could serve different kinds of salads or do a big Salad Bar. You could offer a service project by saying "Dig In. There's Work to do!" Have Primary children sing "Little Purple Pansies."

CHAPTER FIFTEEN

Christmas

RELIEF SOCIETY PARTY

"GIFT SWAP"

A few weeks before Enrichment Night pass out brown lunch sacks to all of the sisters to decorate at home. Sisters will then fill their bag with whatever gifts she would like to give. At Enrichment Night every sister who brings a filled, decorated bag then gets to select another bag to take home. Every bag will be different so its contents will be a fun surprise. The giver remains anonymous unless you want each sister to include a little note inside with a special Christmas message that identifies who she is. You might want to suggest a maximum budget to be spent on the contents.

"SECRET SISTERS"

One month before the Christmas Relief Society Enrichment party have the sisters pick each other's names out of a hat to determine who will be a "Secret Sister" for whom. During the next few weeks the sisters can do all kinds of anonymous service and

make little gifts for the sister whose name she picked out of the
hat. You may want to establish certain guidelines that limit the
dollar amount of spending to encourage sisters to be more creative
and so it won't be a financial burden. At the Christmas party all of
the Secret Sisters will reveal themselves to each other. Often times
there will be sisters who go all out while other sisters don't do very
much. Be sure that it is a voluntary experience so that only the
sisters who really get excited about this idea will participate, while
others who don't want to do it can gracefully slip out.

"CALENDAR CREATOR"

Give each sister a collection of 12 Relief Society stickers for her
to put on her calendars for the new year to remind her what dates
Enrichment Night will be held.

"KEEPING CHRIST IN CHRISTMAS"

In all your preparations for the holidays, help sisters focus on
the birth of Christ and the reason for the season. Share ideas on
how to help children focus on Christ and center Christmas Eve and
Christmas Day activities around the Savior. Make costumes for
families to recreate the Nativity story in the scriptures.

"CHRISTMAS CARDS"

Share ideas on great Christmas cards the sisters can make that
center on the Savior and their families. Collect old Christmas cards
and mail the front to St. Jude's Ranch. They remake them, and use
the profits to help sick children. This can also be a great project to
start in January.

"CAROLING"

Choose several homes or neighborhoods your sisters could visit together and sing a selection of Christmas carols. Bring plates of cookies to give away and have everyone wear Christmas colored clothing and Santa hats. Give copies of music selections so the sisters can take them home and plan a caroling evening with their families in their own neighborhoods.

"PROGRESSIVE DINNER"

If your ward boundaries include your church building you could either begin or end at the building. Hopefully you'll get lucky and find some sisters who live within walking distance to one another so you can have sisters walk to each house after each course. You can have separate houses for hors 'deourves, soup, salad, entrée, and dessert. You may want to limit house visits to just three homes if they're located farther away. If none of the sisters live close enough to each other to make it practical you could host a traveling dinner by using and decorating different rooms in your church building.

"IT'S THE THOUGHT THAT COUNTS"

Offer a fun workshop full of mini-classes on how to make attractive gift baskets, cookie bouquets, inexpensive gift ideas, gifts from the kitchen, card making, gifts children can make, how to ship presents so they don't break in the mail, home-made wrapping paper ideas, how to teach children gratitude, and thank you card ideas. Be sure to offer a lesson that all sisters attend that encourages them to focus their holiday efforts on Christ.

"BOOKMARKS"

Distribute appealing bookmarks for the sisters' Relief Society manual. The bookmark could have the Relief Society statement on it or the dates and themes for next year's Enrichment Nights or even a list of next year's Sundays with which lesson will be taught on a particular day.

"ORNAMENT EXCHANGE"

Find out ahead of time how many sisters would like to participate in this project.

Everyone makes the same number of home-made ornaments and then exchanges them with the others in the group. Have sisters share favorite Christmas memories or talk about any sentimental value they have with certain ornaments.

"CHRISTMAS AROUND THE WORLD"

Focus on international décor, food, music and learning. Have returned missionaries tell about the foreign country where they served, and display items. Don't forget to include the United States!

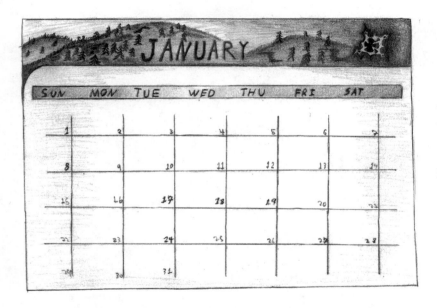

SUN	MON	TUE	WED	THU	FRI	SAT
1	2	3	4	5	6	7
8	9	10	11	12	13	14
15	16	17	18	19	20	21
22	23	24	25	26	27	28
29	30	31				

JANUARY

CHAPTER SIXTEEN
Monthly Traditions

"NEW TO YOU TABLE"

Set out a table where sisters can bring any of their unwanted items from home and anyone is free to take whatever they want. Whatever items still remain at the end of the night can be delivered to Goodwill or Deseret Industries or any other donation organization of your choosing. You could also deliver items to your local Spanish or Vietnamese branch (or whatever special needs branch you have in your area). You can have sisters bring random items each month or designate a different theme each month such as kitchen items, toiletries, children's items, clothing, etc.

"S.O.S. TABLE"

S.O.S. stands for Seek Out Service. Each month one or two organizations are spotlighted so sisters can get ideas for service projects they can get involved in with their families or individually. This is an opportunity to introduce the sisters to ways they can become more involved in their community and reach out to others. You can leave pamphlets or flyers on the table that provide more information with a contact phone number so the sisters can follow through with their interest. You could have one sister make a short presentation each month or simply provide the information on the table so sisters can pick it up some time during Enrichment Night. Organizations you might want to introduce to sisters could include: American Kidney Foundation, Second Harvest, American Cancer Society, local nursing homes they can visit or perform in, local hospitals they can volunteer in, etc.

"FHE PACKET"

It would be great to provide a complete Family Home Evening lesson for sisters who are interested in help with ideas. A packet could be offered for a small cost or sisters could take turns providing copies for each other if the Relief Society budget doesn't allow for copying expenses. A packet could include visual aids, a recipe, songs that coordinate with the selected theme, and even a refrigerator magnet with the scripture for the week!

"QUILTING CORNER"

It would be fun to have a quilt set up somewhere each month that the sisters could work on while they visit with one another. Quilts could be ongoing projects, made as gifts from the Relief Society for new babies, graduating seniors, new brides or sisters in need. Sisters could be encouraged to work for a few minutes each month on the quilt or the Quilt Corner could be an ongoing class offered each month to sisters who might not be interested in the other classes but still want to attend Enrichment Night and enjoy the sisterhood.

"UNFINISHED PROJECTS CORNER"

Some sisters just aren't interested in attending classes but love to sit and chat with their friends during Enrichment Night. The Unfinished Projects Corner allows them that opportunity while keeping their fingers busy. Sisters could be encouraged to bring old craft projects from home that they never finished from previous Enrichment Nights or even miscellaneous mending they never get around to doing. Craft and sewing supplies are provided and sisters can work while they visit with one another.

"RELIEF SOCIETY PHOTO DIRECTORY"

Someone could be assigned to take pictures of any new sisters who have moved in during the last month. Digital cameras make putting together a photo directory a snap! An updated directory could be printed every six months or so. The directory could include phone numbers and addresses of the sisters as well as hours for the closest temple and Family History Center.

"RELIEF SOCIETY SCRAPBOOK"

A sister could be assigned to take pictures each month during Enrichment Night that highlights the classes and activities that are offered. A table could be set up where the sisters could help create scrapbook pages using the photos from previous months. Supplies could be set out on the table and sisters could be encouraged to spend a few minutes working on the pages. This could also be a class offered each month or every few months. Sisters can enjoy each others' company while they use their imagination to create a memorable scrapbook for the Relief Society to enjoy.

"DOOR PRIZES"

Door prizes are fun to use to help solve any problems you might be having with Enrichment Night and to reward positive behavior. For example, if your sisters have a tendency to straggle in late every month you could award door prizes to all the sisters who are there on time. If you want to encourage missionary work with your Relief Society you could offer a little prize to each sister who brings a friend each month. Door prizes could also be offered randomly to add a little excitement for the evening. Prizes don't have to cost much and can even be donated by local vendors. All you have to do is ask!

"THE BABYSITTERS CLUB"

A wonderful tradition is to have the brethren in your ward take turns helping out with the babysitting during Enrichment Night. You could award each brother that serves a little button or certificate that makes him an honorary member of the Babysitters Club. Some time during the year you could even host a little party in honor of all the men who have become members of this prestigious club.

"FRIENDSHIP BASKET"

A friendship basket could be filled and presented each month to a sister whose name has been drawn out of a hat. The recipient then brings the basket filled with new items for the next month's Enrichment Night. The basket could contain random gift items or things that are selected according to a theme such as coordinating with that month's Enrichment Night Theme, Relief Society items, or things that describe the giver and her interests so that the sisters can get to know each other a little better. The basket should not be a financial burden, but an opportunity to simply express friendship and sisterhood.

"BOOK OF MORMON CHALLENGE"

Each month the sisters could be challenged to share a Book of Mormon with a non-member friend. One sister could be selected to give a short report on her experience at the next Enrichment Night.

"SISTER SPOTLIGHT"

Each month a different sister is spotlighted and given a little gift. She stands in front of the group while someone tells all about her favorite things, her accomplishments and talents, and why she is so special in the Relief Society. You could also tell the group all about her and have the sisters guess who they think it is and then present her to the group.

"BIRTHDAY CAKE"

Enrichment Night refreshments each month might include a token birthday cake to be shared by those who are celebrating their birthday during that month.

"MISSIONARY MESSAGES"

A table could be set out each month with stationery, note cards, markers, and so forth, so that the sisters could write letters of encouragement to the missionaries who are serving from the ward. All of the letters could then be mailed individually or together in a special care package from the Relief Society. Similar packages of cards and letters could be mailed to any ward members serving in the military away from home or college students away for the school year.

"RECIPE BOOK"

Each month the recipes for the refreshments served that night could be given to the sisters to add to their collection. A special binder or box could be given to all of the sisters where they can keep all of the recipes together to remember each Enrichment Night.

"WALKING CLUB"

Sisters could be encouraged to exercise each month before Enrichment Night by walking from a certain location to the chapel before the meeting begins. Participation awards could be given in addition to lots of applause for their healthy choices.

"THE LIGHTER SIDE"

Refreshments that are served each month could include something terribly decadent and then a "lighter" version of the same thing could be prepared to help teach sisters how to cook with less fat and calories.

"TASTERS TABLE"

Smaller portions of food could be presented so that sisters could taste a variety of things without having to eat an entire piece. Food choices could go along with the theme that is being presented that night.

"GET TO KNOW YOU TABLE"

Invite all of the new sisters to bring a few items to put on a table that describe themselves and their interests so that all of the other sisters can get to know them a little better.

"VISITING TEACHING INTERVIEWS"

Have the Relief Society presidency and Visiting Teaching Supervisors meet with sisters to discuss needs in the ward and any changes in Visiting Teaching companionships.

"CARPOOL AWARD"

Everyone who drives to Enrichment Night with other sisters gets a little prize. Carpooling encourages sisters to bond, invite and remind each other every month, in addition to saving gas money and the environment!

"LUNCH BUNCH"

Once a month sisters could meet for lunch at a local restaurant that is on the less expensive side of dining. You could also gather for lunch in a different sister's home for a monthly potluck lunch. Sisters might find it fun to bring a brown bag lunch and meet at different parks around town to get to know the area better.

"PARK PALS"

Sisters with young children meet at the park weekly or even

just once a month. You could turn the gathering into a breakfast or lunchtime meal or just meet for fun for an hour.

"SWEATIN' SISTERS"

Sisters can meet at the church or someone's house to exercise together. They can bring different exercise videos or teach one another different routines. During summer months they could meet at someone's pool for water aerobics!

"WALK AND TALK CLUB"

Sisters who are interesting in walking for exercise could meet at a designated location and do it together.

"YOUR NECK OF THE WOODS"

Sisters and their children could plan field trips together to learn more about the sites and history in their area. They could even get group discount tickets if they want to go to a fun place that charges for admission.

"WE ARE DAUGHTERS"

Offer prizes to sisters who can recite from memory the Relief Society Statement. Practice saying it aloud either every Sunday or once a month at Enrichment Night.

"CULTURE CLUB"

This group of sisters could attend movies, theatre, museum lectures, etc. They could receive group discounts and share carpools and babysitting.

"FAMILY HOME EVENING PACKETS"

Sisters who want to share efforts in creating visual aids and fun ideas for family home evening could meet together to work on their projects or have a luncheon where they exchange packets they've already worked on for each other.

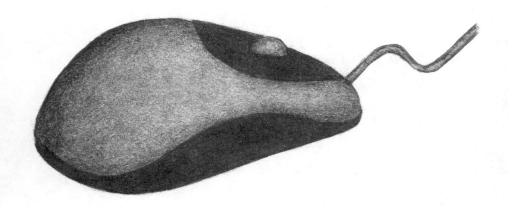

CHAPTER SEVENTEEN

Web Sites with great Enrichment Night ideas

Be sure to use the Internet if you have access to it! Invite the sisters in your ward to share their e-mail addresses with you so you can send out monthly invitations and reminders. You could also provide links for them to go to learn more about topics that will be covered before or after Enrichment Night classes take place, as well as recipes for refreshments that were served. The following are some web site addresses where you can go to get some great ideas for your next Enrichment Night!

- www.lds.org
- www.homemakingcottage.com
- www.mormonchic.com
- www.womenfolk.com
- www.of-worth.com/ea/homemaking.htm
- www.promoms.org/activitease.htm
- www.ldsfiles.com

- http://organizedhome.com
- www.meridianmagazine.com
- www.bellaonline.com
- www.lds-living.com
- www.mormon.org
- www.providentliving.com
- www.homeandholidays.com
- http://lds.about.com/library
- www.dramashare.org/scripts/
- http://wiwi.essortment.com/homefamilyper_rlvf.htm
- www.ineedmoretime.com
- www.michaels.com
- www.joann.com
- www.hometime.com
- www.tightwad.com
- www.fractured.net/
- www.mothersandmore.org
- www.mcphie.org/enrichment
- www.americanmothers.org
- www.powerhomebiz.com/leadership/personal.htm
- www.momscape.com

- www.lds.npl.com
- www.mormon.org
- www.ldstoday.com
- www.lds-index.org
- www.ldsworld.com
- www.ldsliving.com
- www.ldsfriends.com
- www.ldssplash.com
- www.christysclipart.com
- www.mormonmomma.com
- www.deseretbook.com/mormon-life
- www.bevscountrycottage.com
- www.twopeasinabucket.com
- www.primaryetc.com/Rslink.html
- www.nauvoo.com
- www.suite101.com/links.cfm/15768
- www.ldsteach.com

Yahoo groups:
    sister-share
    ldsmomsonline
    Latter_Day_Saint_Women

About the Author and the Illustrator

Trina Bates Boice grew up in sunny California and later braved the cold and snow at Brigham Young University where she earned two Bachelor's degrees. While there she competed on the BYU Speech & Debate team, and BYU Ballroom Dance Team. She was President of the National Honor Society Phi Eta Sigma and ASBYU Secretary of Student Community Services.

Trina also studied at the University of Salamanca in Spain and later returned to serve a full-time mission to Madrid, Spain for the Church of Jesus Christ of Latter-day Saints. She earned a Master's degree from California College for Health Sciences. She worked as a Legislative Assistant for a Congressman in Washington D.C. and wrote a column called "The Boice Box" for a local newspaper in Georgia where she lived for 15 years. She has a real estate license, travel agent license, a Black Belt in Tae Kwon Do, and helps her husband, Tom, with their real estate appraisal and investment companies.

Trina was honored in November 2004 as George Bush's "Points of Light Volunteer" and also received the President's Lifetime Volunteer Service award. She was the "2004 Honor Young Mother of the Year" for the state of California and lives in beautiful Carlsbad with her four wonderful sons. They keep busy with Scouting, all kinds of sports, and are surfer wannabes now that they live closer to the beach. They now brave the cold and snow of Utah together to go skiing and visit family!

Calvin W. Boice III made a flashy entrance into the world by being born at home on Friday the 13th! His parents were trying to get to the hospital, but Calvin just couldn't wait to start his life. So he was born at home by accident. He was named after his grandfather and great-grandfather when his mom gratefully told his dad, "You can name your son anything you want, since you delivered him!"

This is Calvin's first book illustration, but he has won several art contests at school and in the community. He runs on the Cross Country team at Carlsbad High School as a Freshman and is a straight A student. He recently earned his Eagle Scout award, and after climbing Mount Whitney, the highest mountain in the

continental United States, he earned the 50 Miler Award from the
Boy Scouts of America.

In 2004 Calvin earned the Presidential Volunteer Service Award
for his service at church, school, and in Scouting, as well as his
efforts serving with "Operation Appreciation" for the military and
"Supporting Urban Neighborhoods."

He also received the Hometown USA Award presented by the
Keep America Beautiful Foundation. Calvin lives with his family in
Carlsbad, California.